EXPLORING
THE BIG
SOUTH FORK

A Handbook to the National River and Recreation Area

By RUSS MANNING

Mountain Laurel Place
Norris, Tennessee

Printed on Recycled Paper.

Printed in the United States of America

ISBN: 0-9625122-6-5

Unless otherwise noted, photographs are by the author.

Cover: Photo of canoeing courtesy of National Park Service. Horseback riders by Sondra Jamieson. Diffused background map courtesy of the U.S. Geological Survey (U.S. Department of the Interior) and the Tennessee Valley Authority.

Photo page 57 courtesy of NPS.

Published by

Mountain Laurel Place
P.O. Box 3001
Norris, TN 37828

*for the staff of the Big South Fork
National River and Recreation Area*

*who through their dedication and diligent work
protect the natural and historic resources
while providing outdoor recreation and education*

Contents

vi

List of Tables

List of Maps

List of Photographs

Color Photographs

Acknowledgments

Thanks to the National Park Service staff at the Big South Fork National River and Recreation Area for their support in the preparation of this book and especially for the encouragement of Superintendent Bill Dickinson and Park Ranger Management Assistant Ron Wilson. They along with Chief of Interpretation Steven Seven and Chief of Resources Management Ron Cornelius participated in an early planning session that provided direction for the book.

I am especially grateful to Park Ranger Interpreter and local historian Howard Ray Duncan for spending several hours and several phone calls answering my questions. NPS Archaeologist Tom Des Jean answered questions and provided information on the history of the region, including an explanation of gravestone inscriptions. Etta Spradlin, Biological Technician, provided information on the location of cemeteries. Resource Management Specialist Robert Emmott supplied information on the biological communities, and Steve Bakaletz, NPS Biologist, made valuable comments. Anne Malanka, Museum Technician, helped in locating photographs. Forestry Technician Jeanne Richardson and Chief of Maintenance Fred Kelly assisted with information on roads and trails. John Cannon, Chief Ranger, provided advice on park regulations. My thanks to Henrietta Brooks, receptionist and secretary, for fielding my many phone calls and loaning books and papers from the park library.

Many of the NPS staff reviewed all or parts of draft manuscripts and made valuable suggestions. I'm grateful to the following for taking the time to do the review: Bill Dickinson, Steven Seven, Ron Wilson, Robert Emmott, Jeanne Richardson, Howard Ray Duncan, Tom Des Jean, Ron Cornelius, John Cannon, Jim Wiggins (Assistant Superintendent), Brenda D. Coleman (Park Ranger), Sherry Fritschi (Seasonal Ranger), Lisa Collins (Supervisory Park Ranger), and Jerome Flood (Supervisory Park Ranger).

In addition, I am grateful to Dr. Molly F. Miller, Professor of Geology at Vanderbilt University, for taking the time to supply information on the geology of the Big South Fork region and for reviewing my section on geology. I thank Charles P. Nicholson, zoologist with the Tennessee Valley Authority, for helping to construct the list of migratory and resident birds of the Big South Fork. I also thank Bob Wheeley, owner of Cumberland Rapid Transit, for supplying information on paddling the river system and for reviewing that section of the book; Joe Cross, president of the Big South Fork Bicycle Club, for providing information and suggestions on bicycling and mountain biking and for reviewing those sections; Lucy Scanlon, Trailmaster for the annual Big South Fork Competitive xiv

Ride, for providing information and suggestions on horseback riding and for reviewing that section; and Conley Blevins, former interpretive ranger at Blue Heron and a descendent of Jonathan Blevins, for looking over the history section.

I am also grateful to the Stearns Museum; Audney Lloyd, former editor and publisher of the *Scott County News*; and Dr. Benita J. Howell, associate professor of anthropology at the University of Tennessee Knoxville, for various historical photographs as indicated.

Outdoors at the Big South Fork

Because the Big South Fork is a rare combination of recreation area and national river, you'll find more outdoor activities here than at most other units of the National Park System. Visitors to the Big South Fork enjoy everything from hiking and horseback riding to hunting and fishing, from four-wheel drive excursions and bicycling to sightseeing and wildlife watching, from whitewater rafting to picnicking beside the river.

You'll also find here the traces of history, from pioneer farmsteads and log cabins to the remains of large-scale development in the coal and timber industries. You can spend much time here searching out historic sites and old cemeteries or examining the influence of the industrial development that for a time transformed the region. Here, history and the outdoors complement each other, offering a broad experience to stimulate your curiosity and challenge your stamina.

The Big South Fork National River and Recreation (BSFNRRA) was authorized by the U.S. Congress in 1974. The 123,000-acre park, with a few portions yet to be acquired at this writing, encompasses the gorge of the Big South Fork of the Cumberland River and adjacent lands. The park contains the free-flowing river, numerous tributaries, stone arches, waterfalls, rock shelters, early settlement sites, and the forest and wildlife of the Cumberland Plateau in Tennessee and Kentucky. It has long been a gathering place for outdoor enthusiasts, yet there have also

The Big South Fork

been times when the area was threatened. Various plans had proposed a dam for the river near a rapids called "Devil's Jump," which would have flooded the river gorge. Instead, through the efforts of conservation groups and local congressional delegations, the park was established to preserve the geology and the natural communities of the river gorge and to create opportunities for outdoor recreation.

The legislation authorizing the national river and recreation area assigned the responsibility of acquiring lands and developing the park to the U.S. Army Corps of Engineers, with the National Park Service to take over management once the park was established. The Corps purchased land, laid out trails, and constructed recreational facilities, and the NPS took over interim management as pieces were completed. In later years the Corps became limited in its activities because of new federal cost-sharing regulations on its projects, and so although some land still remained to be acquired and park development had not yet been completed, both the Corps and the National Park Service agreed it was time to make the transfer, with the NPS given entire management responsibility. The U.S. Congress authorized the transfer in 1990, and the transfer was officially recognized at the dedication of new park headquarters on August 25, 1991; the ceremony was also a symbolic dedication of the BSFNRRA.

The Big South Fork National River and Recreation Area contains two separate management zones. The Park Service manages the gorge area—approximately 56,000 acres with bare rock walls and steep wooded slopes leading down to the river—as virtual wilderness with no development, except at a few places where legislatively authorized roads wander down to the river. Only activities compatible with the area's wilderness character take place in the gorge area, such as hiking, horseback riding, and paddling the river. Facilities that include a visitor center, campgrounds, and a stables are available on the adjacent plateau surface—about 67,000 acres that make up the rim area of the park. Here visitors can participate in such additional activities as car camping and four-wheel drive and ATV riding.

This handbook serves as an activity guide to these two management zones—the national river area in the gorge and the national recreation area on the plateau. What you'll find first is an introduction to the park that includes a discussion of things you need to know when planning a trip. That's followed by discussions of the geology and biology and the people of the Big South Fork; you'll find activities in these sections related to study of the area, including outings to take. The remainder of the book gives descriptions of the outdoor activities available to park visitors, with recommendations for some of the best routes and locations for experiencing the park.

You'll find here at the BSFNRRA a rich mix of history and the outdoors. The Big South Fork is a special place with much to see and do. Enjoy your stay.

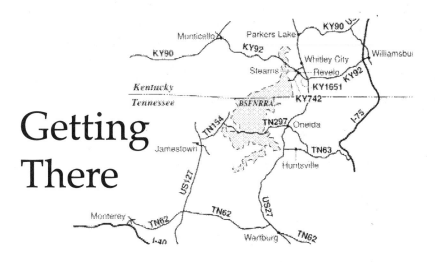

Getting There

The Big South Fork National River and Recreation Area lies atop the Cumberland Plateau west of I-75 between Lexington, Kentucky, to the north and Knoxville, Tennessee, to the south.

You can reach the Tennessee portion of the BSFNRRA by taking TN63 west from the I-75 exit for Huntsville and Oneida. You'll pass through Huntsville and reach US27. Turn north to Oneida where you'll pick up TN297 headed west. You'll enter the park, cross the Big South Fork of the Cumberland River at Leatherwood Ford, and reach a right turn to the park's Bandy Creek Visitor Center on the west side of the river.

If you are traveling from the west in Tennessee, the best approach is east on I-40 to the Monterey exit where you'll pick up TN62 and continue east to a junction with US127. Turn north on US127 to Jamestown; continue north and then turn northeast on TN154. You'll come to TN297 where you'll turn east to reach the Bandy Creek Visitor Center.

Farther east on I-40, you can pick up US127 headed north at the Crossville exit, and even more to the east, you can reach Oneida and the east side of the park by taking US27 north from the Harriman exit. If you're in the Oak Ridge area, take TN62 northwest to Wartburg, where you'll pick up US27 headed north.

The Kentucky portion of the park can be reached from Tennessee by continuing north on US27 from Oneida.

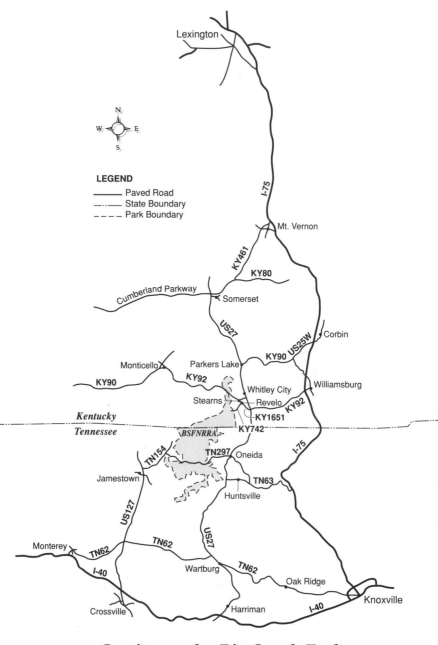

Getting to the Big South Fork

Mileage to the Big South Fork from Surrounding Cities

Asheville, NC	186	Knoxville, TN	80
Atlanta, GA	304	Lexington, KY	261
Birmingham, AL	336	Louisville, KY	339
Charleston, SC	458	Memphis, TN	359
Chattanooga, TN	191	Nashville, TN	150
Cincinnati, OH	339	Richmond, VA	502
Indianapolis, IN	449	Roanoke, VA	336
Jacksonville, FL	635		

If you are coming from the north on I-75 and want to reach the Kentucky portion of the park first, you can exit at Mt. Vernon and take KY461 southwest and then KY80 to Somerset where you'll turn south on US27. Or you can travel farther south on I-75 and exit onto US25W near Corbin and head southwest to a turn west on KY90. You'll travel through the Daniel Boone National Forest and Cumberland Falls State Park and then, at Parkers Lake, turn south on US27. To reach the BSFNRRA from either of these approaches, continue south on US27 through Whitley City to a west turn on KY92 into Stearns (it's also possible to take KY92 west from I-75 at Williamsburg to Stearns, but parts of the highway are steep and winding). Watch for a new visitor contact station that is planned for a location on KY92 east of the Stearns town center. From Stearns, you can take KY1651 to Revelo where you'll turn right on KY742 that becomes Mine 18 Road to the Blue Heron Mining Community in the park. You'll find visitor information there. In Stearns, you can also ride to Blue Heron on the Big South Fork Scenic Railway that operates within the park as a concession.

Traveling from the west in Kentucky, you can go east on the Cumberland Parkway to Somerset and then south on US27 to Stearns. Or you can take KY90 east and then, in Monticello, pick up KY92, which eventually crosses the Yamacraw Bridge over the Big South Fork and leads to Stearns.

Getting There

Planning a Visit

Any visit to the Big South Fork will be more enjoyable and rewarding if you plan ahead. Of course, you don't have to stick to the plan once you get there; it's always fun to do some things spontaneously. But with some planning, you'll be more prepared for the kinds of activities in which you and your group would like to participate.

Contact the park staff to obtain maps and information, either by calling or writing using the phone number and address listed in the back of this book or, when you get there, by going first to the Bandy Creek Visitor Center in Tennessee or, in Kentucky, to the new information center at Stearns, once it's open, or on to Blue Heron. In addition to the maps found in this book, you'll probably find useful the free "Big South Fork Official Map and Guide" that shows the major roads and access points. If you plan to hike or ride horses or mountain bikes, you'll need to purchase a trail map. You can also purchase hiking guides and topographic maps at the Visitor Center and the visitor contact stations in Kentucky.

When you contact the park, ask about the season you wish to visit and current conditions. If the weather has been hot and dry, you may want to plan for shorter hikes. If there has not been much rain, the river may not be suitable for paddling, so you may opt for lazy tubing or swimming in the shallow water. Or if there has been a lot of rain, the river may be too dangerous to paddle.

Ask about the hunting seasons in the fall, winter, and spring. If hunting is going on when you plan to visit, especially big game hunting, you may need to slightly restrict your activities or, at the least, wear bright clothing when you venture into the backcountry.

Once you have gathered the basic information, think about your family or group of friends who will be coming with you and take into consideration their interests and capabilities. You'll find a variety of activities described later in this book from which to choose. And within each of these activities, you can choose from among easy excursions to difficult challenges. So also think about each individual's ability. Will everyone be able to make that 15-mile hike? Will the little ones be able to handle a raft trip on the river?

ACTIVITIES FOR CHILDREN

If your group includes small children, you can still participate in many of the outdoor activities, including picnicking, swimming, wildlife watching, sightseeing, camping, bicycling, fishing, and hiking. When out for a hike or a bicycle ride, you may want to cover the shorter and easier trails.

There are a number of ranger-lead programs that children will enjoy; check the section on Visitor Participation. The Junior Ranger Program is specifically designed for children 3 to 12 years old. The Bandy Creek Campground has a swimming pool, and both the Bandy Creek and Blue Heron Campgrounds have play structures.

Children must be at least six years old to participate in the guided horseback rides from the Bandy Creek Stables, but younger children may participate in wagon rides. Rafting outfitters usually have a minimum age requirement of twelve for the difficult gorge section of the river but generally have no minimums for the float stretches; be aware that even at low water the river has deep holes and swift currents in places. Check with the stables and the various outfitters for suggested trips that would be fun and interesting for younger people.

Families are welcome at the Charit Creek Lodge in the backcountry. And children especially enjoy the train ride on the Big South Fork Scenic Railway from Stearns to Blue Heron.

Planning a Visit

Camping at the Big South Fork

ACTIVITIES FOR THE DISABLED

The park offers opportunities for the physically challenged. The East Rim, Honey Creek, and Devil's Jump Overlooks of the gorge are accessible by wheelchair; other overlooks that are proposed will also be accessible, so check with the Visitor Center. The historic Blue Heron Mining Community has paved walkways, but some get quite steep; universally accessible restrooms are located there.

The boardwalks along the river at Leatherwood Ford are universally accessible. You'll also find restrooms there that can be easily entered. In addition, the John Muir Trail south from Leatherwood Ford for about half a mile has recently been made universally accessible by the Telephone Pioneers of America, an organization of retired telephone workers who devote time to projects that improve the accessibility of public areas for the physically challenged.

Exploring the Big South Fork

Scenic drives, hiking, fishing, rafting, canoeing, camping, and horseback riding are other activities in which persons with various disabilities can participate. Those able to mount a horse may participate in the guided horseback rides offered by Bandy Creek Stables; anyone may participate in wagon rides. Anyone capable of hanging on can usually participate in guided raft trips. The Big South Fork Scenic Railway out of Stearns is universally accessible.

The Bandy Creek Campground in the Tennessee portion of the park and the Blue Heron Campground in the Kentucky portion have accessible campsites. The Bandy Creek Visitor Center with its interpretive programs and restrooms is also universally accessible.

Check with the park staff and with local outfitters for other suggested places and activities.

WHEN TO VISIT

The favorite times to visit the Big South Fork are spring and fall, when the temperatures are mild and you have the special attraction of abundant wildflowers or a forest of red and gold. But the other seasons have their special attractions. In winter, you have better views with leaves off the trees, and you occasionally get to experience a blanket of snow and an icicle-draped gorge; you also don't have to worry about bugs and snakes. And at the height of summer, you can still find cool coves in the depths of the plateau forest or take a refreshing swim in the river at low water.

The Cumberland Plateau region generally has lower temperatures and higher annual precipitation than the adjacent parts of Tennessee and Kentucky, which have lower elevations. The average annual temperature is 55 degrees F and average precipitation is 54 inches.

Average maximum temperatures occur in July and August, while average lowest temperatures occur in January and February.

Prevailing winds from the south and southwest bring moist air from the Gulf Coast that result in rains. Flooding most likely occurs December through March when storm systems dump high-intensity rains. Summer thunderstorms can cause infrequent flash floods. Snowfall averages 17 inches a year, but occurs intermittently and seldom stays around more than a few days before melting.

Planning a Visit

Temperatures and Precipitation for the Big South Fork Region

Month	Avg. Max.	Avg. Min.	Normal	Max Recorded	Min. Recorded	Max. Recorded	Min. Recorded	Normal
	MONTHLY TEMPERATURE (DEGREES F)					MONTHLY PRECIPITATION (INCHES)		
January	45.7	24.5	35.3	74	-22	14.62	1.17	4.91
February	47.6	25.1	36.7	78	-19	12.56	0.50	4.69
March	57.5	33.1	45.0	89	-9	15.26	0.80	5.81
April	68.1	42.1	55.1	96	15	11.73	0.65	4.73
May	76.2	50.3	63.4	95	26	9.16	0.60	4.21
June	83.8	58.1	70.3	104	32	14.55	Trace	4.87
July	84.8	61.3	73.2	103	36	16.82	0.62	5.26
August	84.4	60.7	72.6	103	36	11.85	0.35	3.99
September	79.5	54.7	67.1	102	28	10.76	Trace	3.49
October	69.9	42.2	55.9	92	16	13.17	0.00	2.91
November	57.3	33.5	45.0	85	-8	13.57	0.30	3.90
December	47.8	26.7	37.1	82	-18	13.65	0.22	4.85

Exploring the Big South Fork

WHAT TO BRING

The types of clothing and equipment you need to bring depend on the season in which you visit and the kind of activities in which you choose to participate. If you plan to go horseback riding, bicycling, rock climbing, hunting, backpacking, canoeing, rafting, or other such involved outdoor sports, you should be experienced and know what kinds of clothing and safety equipment to bring with you. If you do not, please contact the park staff or a local outfitter who can give advice on equipment and recommend a level of activity suited to your experience.

Even for just a casual visit, come prepared to experience the park. Wear loose fitting clothing in summer and layers of clothes in winter that you can take off or put on to adjust to the temperature. You should wear walking shoes or hiking boots, which are designed to give sure footing and to support ankles as you walk out to overlooks or take a stroll along the river.

Stopping at Leatherwood Ford Bridge Overlook

Planning a Visit

If you decide to take a longer walk, you'll need a day pack with water, a lunch or snacks, a first aid kit, and rain gear; it rains frequently on the Cumberland Plateau. In summer, throw in some insect repellent and sunscreen. In winter, add extra clothing. All year round, a hat is a good idea. In case you get injured or lost, you should carry along a map, compass, lighter or waterproof matches, fire starter, flashlight with fresh batteries, and a plastic sheet or emergency blanket.

ACCOMMODATIONS

The park has camping and backcountry lodging; check the descriptions for these services in the Outdoor Activities section of this book.

Long-range plans call for park lodges to be constructed, one in Kentucky and one in Tennessee, but those await funding and it may yet be many years before these are available.

You'll find restaurants and lodging in the surrounding communities. Check with the local chambers of commerce for listings; addresses and phone numbers for the chambers are included in the back of this book for Scott and Fentress Counties in Tennessee and McCreary County in Kentucky. Small portions of the park are also in Tennessee's Pickett and Morgan Counties. The BSFNRRA Visitor Center has fact sheets on lodging and restaurants in the region.

BEHAVIOR

While you are here, take care of the park. Leave wildflowers or other plants to grow and reseed and do not collect rocks. Observe wildlife from a distance without harassing them, including snakes, which have a right to be here. Poaching is prohibited.

Refrain from feeding the animals; feeding will cause them to grow accustomed to handouts and to abandon their natural habits, which will endanger their lives. Store food in the trunk of parked cars or, if camping in the backcountry, suspend food bags from a rope between two trees; otherwise mice, raccoons, and skunks may get to your food.

Please don't throw trash on the ground and don't leave pieces of unburned trash in a campfire; garbage along a trail detracts from the experience of the next visitor. You might put aside your natural distaste for cleaning up someone else's mess and pick up what others have thrown down; we can all work to keep our park clean. Glass containers are prohibited from swimming areas along the river.

Leave undisturbed historic and archaeological sites, such as rock shelters, cemeteries, and old housesites. Digging and rummaging around at such sites is in violation of federal law and destroys the archaeological record, making it impossible to piece together the history of the Big South Fork region.

Drinking alcoholic beverages in public areas is prohibited by state law in the Kentucky portion of the park; it is permitted in the backcountry in both states and in picnic areas and campgrounds in the Tennessee portion of the park. But the federal open-container law prohibits the possession of opened containers of alcoholic beverages within a motor vehicle anywhere in the park, including parking lots.

PETS

You may bring pets into the park. Pets must be on a leash at all times, even in the backcountry. Respect other visitors' rights not to be accosted by a barking dog, and do not allow your pet to harass wildlife.

SAFETY AND EMERGENCIES

Take care of yourself while visiting the park. Be especially careful climbing on rocks, hiking along the edge of bluffs, crossing streams, and walking near the river. Do not climb on waterfalls. Unless you are experienced or with an experienced guide, do not participate in such hazardous outdoor activities as climbing and rappelling, caving, canoeing and kayaking, hunting, ATV riding, or horseback riding.

You are expected to take full responsibility for your own safety, keeping in mind that visiting a wilderness setting in which you can at times be far from medical attention is an inherently hazardous activity. You are expected to assume responsibility for knowing where you are going and for not getting lost.

Hunting is allowed in the park during state-designated hunting seasons. Check with the Visitor Center for the dates of the current hunting seasons and wear bright colors, blaze orange recommended, when in the backcountry during hunting seasons.

Planning a Visit

Although backcountry registration is not required, filing a trip report with the park rangers is a good idea. Always let someone know where you are going and what you intend to do.

In an emergency, contact the park rangers at the Bandy Creek Visitor Center (615/879-3625). After hours, you can reach the rangers by contacting the Scott County Sheriff's Office (615/663-2245), no matter in what county you happen to be; tell the dispatcher you need a Big South Fork ranger and give the phone number you are calling from. Telephones are available in the park at Leatherwood Ford, the Blue Heron Mining Community, and the Bandy Creek and Blue Heron Campgrounds.

The nearest hospitals are the Scott County Hospital in Oneida (615/569-8521) and the Fentress County General Hospital in Jamestown (615/879-8171). Ambulance service is available in Scott County (615/569-6000) and Fentress County (615/879-8147) in Tennessee and McCreary County (606/376-5062) in Kentucky.

LOST AND FOUND

Report lost items to the rangers at the Bandy Creek Visitor Center or the Blue Heron Mining Community and to see if the articles have already been turned in. Any article you find while visiting the park should be turned in at one of those locations.

WATER

There was a time in the distant past when a person could kneel and drink from a clean stream in the Big South Fork area. But with people in the backcountry, horses along the trails, and development and farms surrounding the park, that time is gone. All water from streams should be considered unfit for human consumption. If you are in the backcountry and need water, boil water from streams for at least two minutes before drinking; this destroys bacteria and other microorganisms, including Giardia, a flagellate protozoan causing an intestinal disorder called "Giardiasis." There have been confirmed cases in the BSFNRRA. There are also filters and water purifying tablets that can be purchased, but ask your supplier for ones that indeed remove or kill Giardia.

Hiking on the Leatherwood Ford Loop

SNAKES

The Cumberland Plateau has snakes, including the northern copperhead and the timber rattler; people have been bitten by snakes in the BSFNRRA. To be safe, simply watch where you put your feet and hands, and if you must walk through high brush and weeds, explore ahead with a stick. If you do encounter snakes, leave them alone by simply giving them a wide berth. When hiking, wear high-top boots that protect your ankles; thick leggings can give added protection.

If someone in your group is bitten, stay calm and keep the victim calm so the heart rate remains low. Try to pay attention and notice what kind of snake it was so you'll later be able to tell medical personnel; if you do not readily recognize the snake, remember the color and markings so you can describe it. Wash the wound with soap and water if available and if the wound is not bleeding much. If the wound is bleeding heavily, concentrate on controlling the bleeding; the wound can be cleaned later by medical personnel. Apply a band two inches above the bite and two inches below the bite, or if swelling has started, two inches above the swelling and two inches below the swelling, to help contain the venom. Use something like a belt or rubber bands; do not use a tourniquet or a tight band that will stop the blood flow; you should be able to put your finger under the band. Remove rings and watches if bitten in the hand or the arm in case of swelling. Keep the victim warm. Ice applied to the bite site is no longer recommended.

Snake bites usually occur on the arms or legs; immobilize the limb in a functional position by splinting the arm or leg at the elbow or knee to prevent movement that will pump the venom through the body. Elevate the bite site, but always keep it lower than the heart to slow the spread of venom to the heart. Hike out if you are a short distance from your vehicle and then get to an emergency room. If you're a long walk from the trailhead, send someone in the party ahead for help while others carry the victim out or an individual slowly walks the victim out. If the victim has to walk out, you probably won't be able to splint the knee for a leg bite. If it will be more than 30 minutes before the person receives medical attention, then suction the wound using a snake bite kit, but make sure you know how to use the kit properly before starting out on a hike and that it is included in your first aid kit.

INSECTS

During the warm spring and summer days, the gnats, chiggers, and mosquitoes can be a bother. You'll probably want to carry along insect repellent for when the gnats and mosquitoes become incessant. For chiggers, you may want to use the repellent as a preventative, since you won't notice them before it's too late. One way to avoid chiggers is to not sit directly on the ground or a log; carry along a small piece of foam pad to use as a sitting mat for when you take rest breaks or stop for lunch.

Ticks are a special problem because they transmit diseases, including Rocky Mountain spotted fever. The small deer tick can transmit a spirochete that causes Lyme disease. Although tick-related diseases are still relatively rare in the southeastern states, you should remain very conscious of keeping ticks off you and checking for ticks after a hike. If you find a tick that has taken a bite, gently grasp the tick as close to your skin as possible, preferably with tweezers, and pull slowly until the tick releases. Avoid mashing the tick or breaking it off and leaving the head. Later, if a rash appears or you get fever and chills, see a doctor immediately; both Lyme disease and Rocky Mountain spotted fever can be treated with antibiotics.

You might wear long pants and tuck your pants legs inside your socks to keep ticks from getting on your skin. If you wear light-colored clothes, ticks can be easily seen and brushed off. You might also spray your shoetops, socks, and pants legs with repellent to discourage ticks; make sure the repellant is designed for ticks.

There are also occasional hornets, bees, and wasps in virtually any natural setting; you might even see a scorpion. Give them a wide berth. If stung, treat with a sting ointment that you should probably keep in your pack; meat tenderizer can be used to help neutralize the sting venom.

POISON IVY

Poison ivy is the only plant found with frequency in the park that will cause you trouble. An oil from the plant causes a very itchy skin rash. Watch for the three-leaf clusters and try to avoid brushing against it. If you stay to the open trails, you can usually avoid contact. If you venture off trail or encounter an overgrown trail, you'll need to pick your way carefully to avoid the plant. As a vine, poison ivy can climb trees, so also watch where you put your hands. After a hike, wash exposed skin with soap and water to help remove the plant's oils.

HYPOTHERMIA

If you are out for some time in cold and wet weather, you face the danger of hypothermia, the lowering of core body temperature beyond the point at which your body can maintain its own heat. The symptoms are uncontrolled shivering, slurred speech, memory lapse, stumbling, fumbling hands, and drowsiness. Hypothermia can occur in any season and can result in death. Since it is caused by being wet and cold, the treatment is to get dry and warm.

If you are wet and cold, get under some shelter and change into dry clothes. If you begin to experience symptoms, get in a sleeping bag, if available. Drink warm fluids to raise the core temperature of your body. Some people, feeling the symptoms of hypothermia, begin running to increase their body heat, but this should only be attempted in the early stages when you are coherent.

To prevent hypothermia from occurring, stay dry, eat even if you are not hungry so your body will have fuel from which to produce heat energy, and drink water even when you are not thirsty so your body can assimilate your food.

BEARS

Black bears have occasionally been reported in the Big South Fork area and are being considered for reintroduction; they were once more numerous but were driven out by loss of habitat and hunting in the late 1800s and early 1900s. Once bears are reintroduced to the park, it is not likely that you will encounter one because there will only be a few at first and they will be placed far in the backcountry. If you do encounter bears, you should take precautions to not attract or irritate them. But don't overreact, black bears are not nearly as dangerous as, for example, the grizzlies found in the West.

A mother bear is very protective of her cubs. If you encounter a mother with cubs, or a cub alone whose mother is surely nearby, back off. Do not advance on the bears and do not place yourself between the mother and her cubs. If you face a lone bear, observe from a distance and then move on. Do not turn and run, which might cause the bear to run after you; but back off, if you must, to avoid an encounter. Under no circumstances should you feed a bear or leave food for a bear, who would then learn that people carry food and so pose a threat to visitors who come after you. When camping in the backcountry, suspend your food bag on a rope between two trees where a bear cannot get to it.

Access, Facilities, and Services

Roads still used within the BSFNRRA range from state highways and secondary paved roads, through graveled back roads that are still suitable for passenger car traffic, to dirt roads with ruts and holes that should only be attempted by four-wheel drive vehicles. The directions in this book indicate whenever you are directed over a road that might cause trouble for a two-wheel-drive passenger car; you'll find many of these are passable in dry weather but have mudholes in rainy weather.

Whenever the directions indicate a graveled road, you can expect typical problems, such as loose gravel or dirt and an occasional puddle or rock to avoid. Unless some specific cautions are included in the description, you can usually drive the road without getting stuck. But you are expected to use common sense and take responsibility for your own safety and the safety of your vehicle. With heavy rains and the freezing and thawing of winter, ruts can form, roads can collapse, or mudholes can spread. If you are not absolutely sure your vehicle can handle what faces you, back up, turn around, and come back another day when the road has been repaired.

While driving the roads of the BSFNRRA, watch for crossing wildlife and give them the right-of-way. You'll occasionally see a deer bounding across a road; where there's one, there are others, so slow down and watch out for the next one to come across. Also watch for horse

Gravel and dirt roads penetrate the backcountry

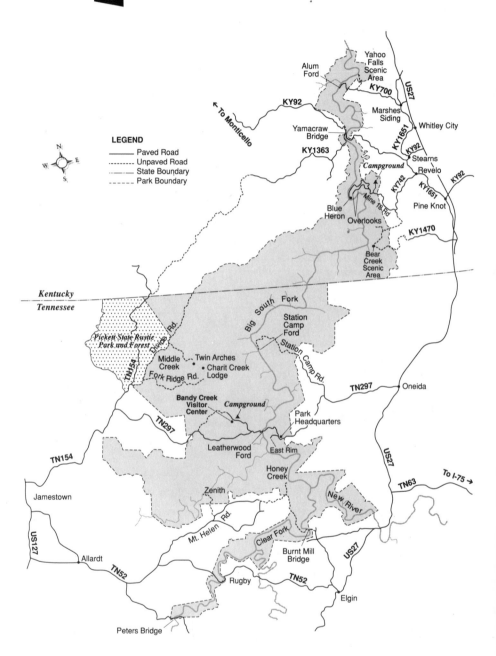

Yahoo
Falls
Scenic
Area

Alum
Ford

KY700

US27

KY92

Marshes
Siding

Whitley City

←To Monticello

Yamacraw
Bridge

KY1651

KY92

LEGEND

N
W E
S

———— Paved Road
············· Unpaved Road
—··—··— State Boundary
— — — — Park Boundary

KY1363

Campground

Stearns

Revelo

KY742

KY1651

KY92

Blue
Heron

Mine 18 Rd.

Overlooks

Pine Knot

KY1470

Bear
Creek
Scenic
Area

Kentucky
Tennessee

Big South Fork

Station
Camp
Ford

Pickett State Rustic
Park and Forest

Divide Rd.

Middle
Creek

TN154

Fork Ridge Rd.

Twin Arches
• Charit Creek
Lodge

Station Camp Rd.

TN297

Oneida

Bandy Creek
Visitor
Center

Campground

TN297

Park
Headquarters

TN154

Leatherwood
Ford

East Rim

US27

Honey
Creek

TN63

To I-75 →

Jamestown

Zenith

New River

Mt. Helen Rd.

Clear Fork

US127

Allardt

TN52

Rugby

Burnt Mill
Bridge

US27

TN52

Elgin

Peters Bridge

Access Points within the BSFNRRA

Exploring the Big South Fork

crossings; horse trails cross TN297 west of Bandy Creek Road, for example. You should always be on the lookout for hikers, horses, and bicycles on the roads.

Following are brief descriptions of the major access points in the park and the facilities and services you'll find there. Refer to the accompanying map to confirm the location of these access points within the park.

BANDY CREEK

The Bandy Creek Visitor Center is probably the best place to begin your visit to the BSFNRRA. Here you'll find books and maps about the area and park rangers who are eager to give advice and directions. You can also get a list of outfitters who can take you on the river by raft and canoe and into the backcountry by horse and mountain bike. The complex at Bandy Creek also has a campground with electric and water

Bandy Creek Visitor Center

hookups for RVs and tent campsites, group camps, a swimming pool, stables for boarding horses, horses for rent on guided trips, wagon rides, picnic areas, and trails for hiking, mountain biking, and horse riding. The Visitor Center complex lies north of TN297 on the west side of the river. Here TN297 and the Bandy Creek Road pass through Scott State Forest, a state of Tennessee inholding within the park boundaries.

LEATHERWOOD FORD

Where TN297 crosses the Big South Fork lies the Leatherwood Ford River Access. This is the primary takeout and putin for canoeing and rafting the river. Restrooms, picnic areas, boardwalks at the river's edge, and hiking trails along both sides of the river are there for your use. You'll see there the old low-water Leatherwood Ford Bridge below the new highway bridge; during flood periods the old bridge is often underwater. The name "Leatherwood," some say, comes from the Leatherwood shrub which has strong leather-like bark and is found frequently at Leatherwood Ford, while another source says that the

Leatherwood Ford River Access

name was brought by the Blevinses, one of the early families who settled the region and many of whom had lived on Leatherwood Creek in Virginia. The river access is on the east side of the river only one mile east down TN297 from the Bandy Creek Road leading to the Visitor Center.

EAST RIM

A half mile inside the east entrance to the park on TN297, you'll pass by the BSFNRRA headquarters complex with the main headquarters building located back from the road to the northeast; this headquarters area is not a visitor contact point. A paved road to the southwest leads 0.7 mile to the East Rim Overlook. Watch for the sign directing your turn left; another paved road off TN297 leads to a maintenance area. About halfway along the East Rim Overlook Road, you'll pass the East Rim Trailhead, where hiking trails begin; one to the south leads to Sunset Overlook. A proposal calls for the hiking trail to also become a biking trail connecting the two overlooks.

STATION CAMP EAST

North of where TN297 crosses the park in Tennessee, you can descend to the Station Camp River Access on the east side of the river across from the mouth of Station Camp Creek. Outside of the park, on the east side of the river, take the Station Camp Road west where TN297 makes a right angle turn at the Terry and Terry Store. The paved road becomes graveled, but it is scheduled to be paved all the way to the river at some later date. You'll enter the park and pass the Station Camp East Trailhead at 4.4 miles, where horse trails begin and hiking trails are proposed, and then pass a side road leading to an equestrian camp. Farther along the road an additional trailhead is proposed to provide more access for hiking and horse trails. You'll pass parking for the rock structures called the "Chimneys" and finally reach the river at 8.1 miles. Hiking and horse trails enter the river access area. Fording the river here at low water provides access to trails on the west side of the river; do not attempt at high water. This is also an access point for paddlers and is used for fishing, swimming, and picnicking.

Access, Facilities, and Services

Station Camp Ford at low water

BURNT MILL BRIDGE AND HONEY CREEK

The southern portion of the park contains the Burnt Mill Bridge River Access. Take US27 south from Oneida. At 10 miles, turn west on Mountain View Road. At 1.6 miles from the turn, signs direct you right, then left, and at 3.8 miles at a four-way intersection, right on a small side road. You can also reach this point if you are coming from the west on TN52 or from the south on US27; on TN52 turn north a half mile west of Elgin and go 3.3 miles to the four-way intersection and go straight ahead on the small side road. A half mile down this side road, bear left onto a gravel road, and then in another 0.4 mile, you'll cross Burnt Mill Ford Bridge. You'll find parking on the west side of the river. The bridge is deteriorating and scheduled for replacement; it's recommended that you do not drive across the bridge in a large vehicle, such as a bus or large RV, until a new bridge is erected.

You have river access here to the Clear Fork River, a primary tributary of the Big South Fork. You can picnic beside the river, go for a swim, or take a walk on a loop trail.

From here you can also continue on the road, now dirt, 3.4 miles and turn right when the road forks to reach the Honey Creek Trailhead/ Overlook; the road from Burnt Mill Bridge to the Honey Creek turnoff can be rough but is usually passable to passenger cars, except maybe in winter when it gets muddy. It is also possible to reach Burnt Mill Bridge along this road from the west by turning on the Mt. Helen Road 7.1 miles west of Rugby on TN52; this is the route used by large vehicles to get to the Burnt Mill Bridge River Access and so avoid crossing the old bridge.

After making the turn into the Honey Creek area, you'll pass the trailhead on the right for the loop hike through the area and then continue another 0.8 mile to the Honey Creek Overlook of the Big South Fork. Picnicking is available here also.

RUGBY AND PETERS BRIDGE

On TN52 between US27 and US127, you'll pass through Rugby, an historic community outside the park boundaries. In the area, you'll find the Gentlemen's Swimming Hole Trail leading into the BSFNRRA along

Burnt Mill Ford Bridge

the Clear Fork River. Also in the vicinity is river access to White Oak Creek on the east and the Clear Fork River on the west; at the Brewster Bridge crossing of the Clear Fork, you'll find picnicking and swimming. A BSFNRRA visitor information station will eventually be located near Rugby off TN52; proposed development includes a major campground, trailheads, and a picnic area. The community itself is an interesting side attraction, a pre-1900 Victorian community where you'll find lodging and historic tours. A rebuilding of the historic Tabard Inn at Rugby has been proposed to serve as the BSFNRRA Tennessee lodge, but so far funding for the lodge has not been found. TN52 is to be rerouted around Rugby to avoid commercial traffic from having to drive through the community, so watch for a change in roads.

About 9 miles west of Rugby on TN52, you can turn south on the Peters Ford Road 4.5 miles to the Peters Bridge crossing of the Clear Fork River. You'll find a picnic area and river access there. Eventually a hiking trail will follow the river north.

MIDDLE CREEK

West of the Bandy Creek Visitor Center, outside the park, you can head north on TN154; 2 miles from the intersection with TN297, turn east on the graveled Divide Road into the Middle Creek area. At 0.7 mile from the turn, you'll reach the Middle Creek Trailhead where hiking trails begin. Continue another 3.2 miles along the road and turn right for 2 miles on another gravel road to the Twin Arches Trailhead for a hike to Twin Arches.

Just 0.3 mile beyond the Middle Creek Trailhead, you can also turn right on Fork Ridge Road. You'll soon pass the Middle Creek Equestrian Trailhead on the left; a new horse camp is planned for a site nearby. At 1.1 miles along Fork Ridge Road, you'll reach the Sawmill Trailhead for more hiking trails. Staying with Fork Ridge Road as it bears to the left, you'll reach the end of the road in another 3.5 miles where you'll find horse and hiking trails that lead down to Charit Creek Lodge that sits at the junction of Charit Creek with Station Camp Creek. This is a backcountry lodge that provides food and accommodations in a primitive setting; reservations are needed.

BLUE HERON

For the Kentucky portion of the park, the best place to begin is the Blue Heron Mining Community. This is a resurrected historic mining community open for sightseeing. The giant tipple that the miners used to separate the coal into different sizes dominates the scene. The tram bridge still spans the river and provides access to hiking trails on the west side. Building-like structures depict the community as it once was. You'll also find here restrooms, river access for boating and swimming, picnic tables, horse and hiking trails, various historic exhibits, and an information booth where you can purchase books and maps about the park.

If you are headed north on US27 from the Tennessee portion of the park, you'll cross the state line and continue to a left turn on KY1651 at Pine Knot. You'll make a sharp right turn in town and continue another 2.6 miles to Revelo where you'll turn left on KY742. KY1651 continues on to the community of Stearns; so if you are coming from the north,

Train Depot at Blue Heron

head south on US27 to a right turn on KY92; in 1.3 miles, at Stearns, bear left on KY1651, and then in 1.1 miles turn right on KY742. From the beginning of KY742, you'll pass the left turnoff for the Bear Creek Scenic Area at 3.2 miles, and the highway then becomes the Mine 18 Road. At 5 miles, you'll pass a side road on the right leading to the Blue Heron Campground that provides for tent and trailer camping. At 5.8 miles, a side road to the left leads out to the Devil's Jump and Blue Heron Overlooks. Once you get to the Blue Heron Mining Community at 8.2 miles, you'll pass the Depot/Exhibit area and the old Blue Heron Tipple to a parking area.

You can also reach the mining community by taking the Big South Fork Scenic Railway out of Stearns; when the train arrives at Blue Heron, a giftshop and a snack bar are open. Future plans call for the Kentucky District Office of the park to be moved from the town center of Stearns to a location on KY92 closer to US27 where it will have a visitor information station; so once this new contact point is established, you might want to approach Blue Heron along KY92 into Stearns even if you're coming from the south, instead of turning at Pine Knot.

BEAR CREEK

The Bear Creek Scenic Area is one of the out-of-the-way places. Here you can walk a short trail to the Bear Creek Overlook of the Big South Fork Gorge or a short loop to see Split Bow Arch. There's also a picnic table and grill. On KY742 on the way to the Blue Heron Mining Community, watch for the Bear Creek Scenic Area sign 3.2 miles from Revelo. Turn left. The road turns to gravel in 1.8 miles and becomes a one-lane road. At 2.0 miles bear right at a scenic area sign. At 2.3 miles, you'll reach a junction where if you were to turn right for 0.8 mile you'd find a new equestrian camp scheduled to open in 1994. Turn left at the junction to get to the scenic area. At 3.3 miles you'll reach an overlook for the Split Bow Arch just off the road to the right. Continue to the scenic area parking on the right at 3.5 miles. Another 0.3 mile down the Bear Creek Road, you'll find more parking for access to the Bear Creek Gage Road, just beyond, that leads down to the river in half a mile (only open to hikers and horses); this parking area is the proposed Bear Creek

Meandering Big South Fork from Bear Creek Overlook

Trailhead, which will provide access to horse trails in the area. The Bear Creek Road continues on from the scenic area for 7.0 miles out to US27 as KY1470, which provides a shorter route if you're coming from the Tennessee portion of the park; be aware the graveled road passes through a small creek at one location, which could be flowing if there has been a recent rain. Original plans for the park called for a lodge to be built near the Bear Creek Scenic Area, but the proposal has stalled because of the lack of good roads and utilities.

YAMACRAW

North of the Blue Heron area of the park, you can continue west on KY92 from Stearns 5.3 miles to the Yamacraw Day Use Area on the east side of the river at the Yamacraw Bridge crossing of the Big South Fork. You can also reach this area east on KY92 from Monticello. This region gets its name from an Indian tribe that once lived there. The day use area

provides picnicking and access to the Sheltowee Trace National Recreation Trail and, on the river's west side, a river access point. The river
area north of Yamacraw is legislatively defined as adjacent area; the
gorge area is defined as stopping at the KY92 crossing of the river.
South of the highway bridge, look for the old Kentucky and Tennessee
Railroad bridge across the river; at the time the Stearns Company built
the bridge in 1907, it was the largest concrete railroad bridge in the
South—575 feet long with five arches. To get to the bridge you can turn
south on KY1363 on the west side of the river for 0.7 mile to view the
bridge, but in summer with leaves on the trees, it's difficult to get a look;
there's a turnout on the left where you can walk to the top of the bridge,
but do not walk out on the bridge. For a better view, turn down under the
highway on the east side of the river at the day use area on KY92, and
from the end of the graveled parking lot, follow the path that heads into
the woods and make your way along the river until you can see the
bridge; you should attempt this only when the river is at low water

*The K&T train crossed the Big South Fork on the bridge at Yamacraw
(Courtesy of Stearns Museum)*

Access, Facilities, and Services

because the trail disappears and you have to scramble some along the bank of the river or push your way through brush, so take care. The park staff has proposed rerouting the Sheltowee Trace to follow this route south from Yamacraw and to cross the river on the K&T Bridge; so at some future time there may be an established trail to the bridge and you'll be able to walk across.

YAHOO FALLS AND ALUM FORD

Farther north, you can reach the Yahoo Falls Scenic Area by taking KY700 west from US27 just north of Whitley City. You'll travel through Marshes Siding and cross KY1651, which you could take north from Stearns to reach this junction. Continuing on KY700, you'll soon enter the Daniel Boone National Forest and then at 4.0 miles turn right on a gravel road. If you were to keep going straight, you'd arrive at the Alum Ford River Access on the Big South Fork, which has picnicking, river access, primitive camping, and additional access to the Sheltowee Trace. After making the turn on the gravel road, it's 1.5 miles down to the Yahoo Falls Scenic Area. There's a large picnic area with hiking trails that begin at the backside of the one-way loop and lead to overlooks and Yahoo Falls, the tallest waterfall in the BSFNRRA. From the overlooks, you'll see that at this northern location the waters of Lake Cumberland reach up into the river gorge, backed up by Wolf Creek Dam far downstream on the Cumberland River.

The
Geology

The New River and the Clear Fork join in Tennessee to form the Big South Fork of the Cumberland River, which then flows north across the Cumberland Plateau to join the main stem of the Cumberland River in Kentucky. Along the way, the Big South Fork plows a steep-walled gorge that in places reaches 600 feet in depth. The surrounding landscape is also a geologic wonder on the smaller scale, with natural arches, chimneys, waterfalls, and rock shelters.

THE RIVER GORGE

The Big South Fork Gorge is the centerpiece of the national river and recreation area, and from most overlooks in the park you can see evidence of the geological forces that continue to create the gorge. One of the best overlooks, and easiest to get to, is the Devil's Jump Overlook on the Overlooks Road off the Mine 18 Road that leads down to the Blue Heron Mining Community in Kentucky. In Tennessee, the easiest to get to is the East Rim Overlook off TN297 on the east side of the river, but the rock is not much exposed there. A better one for studying the gorge geology in Tennessee is the Honey Creek Overlook; follow the directions for the Burnt Mill Bridge in the previous section on Access and continue to the Honey Creek area on a dirt road to a right turn that leads to the overlook; the road could be muddy in winter.

Big South Fork Gorge from Angel Falls Overlook

From these overlooks, across the gorge and even to the rear if you had a view not blocked by trees, you'll be looking off across the top of the Cumberland Plateau. You'll see hills and maybe even mountains in the distance, referred to as the "Cumberland Mountains," that stand on this northern region of the Plateau. Even so, you would think you stand on the general lay of the land. But in fact, you are on a tableland that rises a thousand feet above the surrounding regions.

This tableland resulted from a long history of geological change. For millions of years, a shallow sea covered what is now Tennessee and Kentucky. Multitudes of animals lived in the waters. When they died, their skeletons and shells were broken and scattered by the waves and eventually settled on the sea floor where the fragments were compacted and cemented together to form limestone.

Then about 320 million years ago, the land to the east rose. Rains falling on these new mountains formed rivers, many flowing west from these Appalachian highlands. The rivers and streams brought with them uncountable tons of sand and mud eroded from the mountains. This debris settled out as the water met the shallow inland sea and slowed, the streams fanning out to form a great delta system where lush vegetation grew. Occasionally, the delta settled under its own weight and allowed the sea to invade and deposit its layers of silt, which now contained only a few shells since the frequent coverings of delta mud suppressed life in the sea. For about 10 million years the rivers and the sea deposited their silt and mud along this shoreline in the area that was to become the Cumberland Plateau.

Then began a final episode of Appalachian mountain building to the east that provided additional material to be carried by the streams flowing west to the sea. Geologists think the uplift, called the "Allegheny Orogeny," resulted from a collision of the African and North American continental plates, occurring at the slow pace of geologic time. The force of this compression caused a wrinkling and warping of the surface rock that created new mountains to the east.

The erosion of these new mountains occurred so quickly that the rivers became choked with the sediment. But the material eventually worked its way through and covered the whole delta area as a layer of sand and gravel over a hundred feet thick. When the deposition slowed, vegetation once more spread across the delta. But later, as the shoreline settled once again, the sea reinvaded and dropped its silt, burying the vegetation. This cycle of mountain building to the east followed by erosion and deposition of sediment in what is now the Plateau region repeated in several pulses over millions of years during a time geologists call the "Pennsylvanian Period" and may have extended into the Permian Period to as late as 250 million years ago.

Under the increasing weight, these piled-up layers consolidated into rock. Water between the grains squeezed out, and minerals that precipitated from the water cemented together the mud and silt and sand and gravel and organic matter. These became layers of shale, siltstone, clay, sandstone, and coal. The hundred-foot thick sand and gravel layer first laid down following the initiation of the Allegheny Orogeny was tightly cemented, forming a tough Pennsylvanian sandstone called the "Rockcastle Conglomerate."

Later, probably much later, the area that is now the Plateau rose high above sea level in a process of secondary uplift called "isostatic adjustment." In the process, uplift occurs as the weight of overlying layers is removed by erosion and less dense rock below is forced upward by surrounding dense rock. In the Plateau area, rain and the resulting streams swept away sedimentary deposits, nearly leveling the region; the weight from above was thus reduced and the land rose.

There were several intervals of secondary uplift in which as the mountains rose they were eroded down again until the Rockcastle Conglomerate was uplifted and exposed. This resistant sandstone conglomerate then slowed the erosional process. Above the conglomerate, streams swept away the more easily removed rock and soil, creating the tableland known today as the Cumberland Plateau. Some of this hard sandstone eroded also, but much of it still remains as a cap to the Plateau, covering less resistant rock layers below.

The overlook platform you stand on at one of the river overlooks straddles a portion of the Rockcastle Conglomerate at the edge of the Big South Fork Gorge. Without this capstone, the Plateau would have long ago eroded away. It is this Pennsylvanian sandstone that has saved the Cumberland Plateau, a long linear tableland running northeast to southwest that still stands 2000 feet above sea level and a thousand feet above adjacent regions to the east and west.

When you have the opportunity to view the conglomerate close up at various locations, you'll notice different features. In vertical cliffs you'll occasionally see concave shapes in the rock tens of feet across and lined with quartz pebbles or flattened chunks of mud; these are the outlines of river channels of more than 300 million years ago that were later filled with sand. Places that have inclined layers abutting other slanting layers are where sand accumulated against the sloping sides of sandbars on the bottom of ancient rivers; such layers generally slope downstream, which is how geologists know the rivers flowed south-southwest.

Some of the cement that holds the sand grains together to make the sandstone contains iron oxide which gives the rock a yellow, orange, or brown tint. The cement sometimes concentrates in dark lines that are more resistant to erosion than even the sandstone, and so it stands out in filigree patterns in a sandstone wall.

Flattened holes an inch or two across are voids that were once filled with chunks of mud eroded from the banks of the ancient streams. Indentations and pits on the rock surface are more recent features caused by uneven erosion in this resistant capstone.

Once the rains and resulting streams had eroded down to this Rockcastle Conglomerate, the water gathered into cracks in the sandstone that had formed in the rock when it was lifted high above sea level. The sandstone is less resistant along these cracks and so erodes more easily, forming conduits for the streams of water to reach the less resistant layers below. Several of these streams converged to form the Big South Fork. Small tributary streams still slowly work through the resistant sandstone. Larger tributaries have recently penetrated the sandstone and now are more easily eroding the underlying layers. The river itself, with its large volume of water and erosive power, has removed much of the underlying rock, carving the gorge you see before you.

Although the plateau surface gave way to the downward erosion of the river, the Pennsylvanian sandstone at the edges resisted the river's lateral forces. You'll see the sandstone on your side of the river, but also

View from Devil's Jump Overlook

look across the gorge to the other side. At places like the Devil's Jump and Honey Creek Overlooks, you'll see exposed blocks of sandstone at the rim. This layer of sandstone resisted being washed away when the river was forming, otherwise the river would have spread out into a wide stream. Instead the river's erosion proceeded downward into less resistant rock layers, creating a gorge hundreds of feet deep.

If you look closely at the wall on the other side of the gorge, you can perhaps see some of the other rock layers below the Pennsylvanian sandstone—shale, coal, other sandstone that is less resistant. In most places, these other layers are hidden by a forested slope at the base of the gorge wall. When you get down to the river and walk some of the trails below the gorge rim, you'll occasionally see the layers of shale and coal in the rock walls. Rarely you'll see limestone, for only in the deepest parts of the gorge to the north has the river begun to reach limestone layers, deposited before the delta system formed.

Although the sandstone at the rim has resisted erosion, the effects of the process can be seen in the irregular rock faces. In places the sandstone has gradually eroded, with pieces as big as houses giving way and slipping and sliding down the slope. Some pieces break off under their own weight, tumbling into the gorge to land at the river's edge or to splash into the river itself. From your overlook and later while walking along the river, you can see large blocks of stone sitting at the river's edge. Smaller boulders make up a rubble zone along the river. Boulders that have landed in the river cause the water to wash and swirl around them, creating such rapids as the Devil's Jump and making the Big South Fork one of the best streams for whitewater rafting and canoeing in the Southeast.

Today the Big South Fork continues making the gorge deeper. If you are visiting on a summer day when little rain has fallen, you'll see a placid stream with deep green pools and wonder how it could have formed such a deep gorge. But if you stand at an overlook during the rainy

Big South Fork just below confluence

The Geology

Devil's Jump Rapids

seasons in winter and spring, and if the rain has come recently, you'll see a dark, fast-moving river, brown with the soil and silt and rock it carries downstream. Later while walking along the river, you'll see debris lodged in the trees ten or twenty feet over your head by the occasional flood that comes sweeping downriver.

The Big South Fork is a vibrant place where geologic forces have created, and continue to create, a magnificent river gorge. But, in addition, these forces have also created small-scale geologic wonders for you to seek out.

NATURAL ARCHES

The Big South Fork region may have more natural arches than any other region in the eastern U.S. The tally is not yet complete because hikers and horseback riders discover small arches from time to time as they continue to explore the backcountry. But it's clear at this point that the Big South Fork is one of the primary places in the East for natural arches. Two of the park's best are the Twin Arches in the Middle Creek area in Tennessee and Split Bow Arch in the Bear Creek area in Kentucky.

To get to Twin Arches, travel north on TN154 on the west side of the park. Just before reaching Pickett State Rustic Park turn east on the graveled Divide Road into the Middle Creek area. In about 4 miles, turn right on another gravel road that leads 2 miles to the Twin Arches Trailhead. It's then a 0.7-mile walk to the arches.

Natural arches are found frequently in the Big South Fork region at the edges of the tableland surface, where the resistant Rockcastle Conglomerate slowly succumbs to erosion. This is the same Pennsylvanian sandstone that has focused erosion downward, creating the deep river gorge. Arches form at the Big South Fork because the resistant sandstone is able to support its own weight when layers below erode away.

Arches form by a number of geologic processes. One of the most common methods is headward erosion—where the head of a gully erodes up a slope until it encounters the sandstone at the ridgeline. The sandstone cap rock resists falling apart, and so the rain and seeping

The Geology

South Arch of Twin Arches

water proceed to erode under and through underlying sandstone, eventually opening a hole in the ridge and leaving a layer of the resistant sandstone suspended above ground.

Headward erosion, probably on both sides of the ridge, is the process that created the North and South Arches of the Twin Arches complex. These two nearly aligned arches are massive; the North Arch has a span of 93 feet and a clearance of 51 feet, and the South Arch, the largest in the Big South Fork, has a span of 135 feet and a clearance of 70 feet.

Notice these arches occur on a very narrow spur of the plateau that is slowly eroding. There was likely once an arch beyond the South Arch; if you explore south from the arch, you'll see a gap in the ridge with a mound in between that is probably the remains of the collapsed arch. If you climb the stairway to the top of the Twin Arches complex and then climb to the very top of South Arch (you need to be somewhat agile), you'll get a good view showing the gap in the ridge where the older arch once stood. As the slow process of erosion continues, the South and North Arches will eventually collapse, causing the edge of the plateau to recede. Other arches will likely form farther back along the way.

In addition to the two main arches, the Twin Arches complex includes two tunnels. At the south end of South Arch, you'll find the West Tunnel, on the west side. This 88-foot long tunnel took shape through the widening of a joint, where erosion has opened a crack in the rock. You'll find the East Tunnel on the east side, between the North and South Arches under the wooden stairs to the top. This much smaller passage was most likely formed by groundwater flowing through an area of weak cementation and eroding a hole in the rock. So within the Twin Arches complex, you'll find arches and tunnels created by three different geologic processes.

The Split Bow Arch in Kentucky was likely formed by a combination of headward erosion and widening of a joint. To get to the arch, head down KY742 toward the Blue Heron Mining Community and turn left toward the Bear Creek Scenic Area and follow the signs 3.3 miles to an overlook on the right for Split Bow Arch. To get a better look, you'll need to hike the trail to the arch, so continue another 0.2 mile down the road

Split Bow Arch

to parking for the Bear Creek Overlook. You'll find the trailhead for the 0.7-mile Split Bow Arch Loop at the northern end of the parking area. You'll reach the arch halfway along the loop; walk counterclockwise.

Just before the arch, the trail enters a narrow passageway between rock walls, and then just beyond, you'll find a huge hole in the wall on your left creating the large Split Bow Arch above. Headward erosion worked its way up the slope and eventually wore the hole in the sandstone, while the widening of a joint (the narrow passageway the trail followed) separated the top of the hole from the rock wall behind to form the arch.

There are other well-known arches in the national river and recreation area. Needle Arch stands off the Slave Falls Loop Trail in the Middle Creek area, and Wagonwheel Arch sits on the north side of the Mine 18 Road just before the turnoff to the Blue Heron Campground. There are also many small unnamed arches throughout the park—on the Grand Gap Loop, in the ridge above Charit Creek, just off the trail that follows Laurel Fork near the Middle Creek area, in the ridge above Laurel Fork, up Andy Creek from Station Camp Creek, a rare double arch on land that is still private property but within the southern boundary and so will be acquired eventually. Some of these are quite remote; but watch for them and others as you explore the backcountry.

CHIMNEYS

Along an eroded slope, you'll occasionally see a rock sitting on a pedestal of dirt. While rain has washed away the surrounding earth, the rock has sheltered the dirt beneath it, creating the pillar formation. A similar process at work in the Big South Fork region creates large rock structures called "Chimneys."

To view some chimneys, take the Station Camp Road off TN297 on the east side of the river; it becomes a gravel road at this writing, but it is scheduled for paving. As you follow the road down toward the river, watch for a parking area for the Chimneys on the right at 7 miles from the TN297 turnoff. Two of the 10-15 foot rock columns stand on the left side of the road; they have long been a landmark in the area.

You can climb up to the chimneys to get a better look. You'll see they

The Geology

Chimney on Station Camp Road

are topped with rock stained orange-brown with a small amount of iron deposits. This resistant rock has protected the more easily eroded underlying layers while the surrounding unprotected rock has eroded away more quickly, leaving the chimney-like structures.

WATERFALLS

Cascading streams and falls of water can be found throughout the Big South Fork area. The most impressive is Yahoo Falls in Kentucky. Just north of Whitley City, turn west on KY700. At 4.0 miles turn right on a gravel road and travel another 1.5 miles down to the Yahoo Falls Scenic Area. At the one-way loop, stay to the right and pass through a picnic area to the backside of the loop, where you'll see the trailhead on the right. Then walk the 0.8-mile Topside Loop to get to the waterfall. You'll need to visit winter or spring when there is plenty of water; late summer and early fall, the creek that forms the waterfall can be virtually dry.

The drop of 113 feet makes this the tallest waterfall in the Big South Fork area and the tallest in Kentucky. What also makes this an especially scenic place is the large rock shelter behind the waterfall. Both the height of the waterfall and the hollowed out rock behind are due, once again, to the presence of the Rockcastle Conglomerate.

This Pennsylvanian sandstone at the lip of the waterfall resisted breaking off as the falls formed; so erosion proceeded downward into underlying layers, creating the great height of the waterfall and the surrounding wall of a plunge basin. The less-resistant rock layers that then formed the back wall of the basin, being more vulnerable to erosion, began to wear away. As a hole took shape behind the waterfall, the rock above fractured and fell away. The cavity grew larger until it reached the more resistant sandstone above that would not fracture as readily and so now forms the roof of the rock shelter.

A tall waterfall with an amphitheater-like cavity behind is typical for waterfalls in the entire Cumberland Plateau region. Yahoo Falls at the Big South Fork is one of the best examples. Another is Slave Falls in the Tennessee portion of the park. To get to this 60-foot waterfall, take TN154 north on the west side of the park and then turn east on the

Yahoo Falls

Exploring the Big South Fork

Slave Falls

The Geology

Boulder House Falls on Honey Creek Loop

graveled Divide Road into the Middle Creek area. In one mile, turn right on Fork Ridge Road and drive another 1.1 miles to the Sawmill Trailhead where you can walk the Slave Falls Loop clockwise 1.3 miles to a view of Slave Falls.

You'll find other, smaller, waterfalls as you explore the BSFNRRA. There's Fall Branch Falls on the John Litton Farm Loop out of the Bandy Creek area, Boulder House Falls and Honey Creek Falls on the Honey Creek Loop west of the Burnt Mill Bridge Access, Dick Gap and Big Spring Falls south from the tram bridge on the west side of the river at Blue Heron.

One you'll surely hear about is Angel Falls, north of the Leatherwood Ford crossing of the Big South Fork on TN297. Angel Falls was in fact a low waterfall in the river, but in the 1950s some individuals dynamited the falls in an attempt to improve navigation for fishing boats, with little success. If you walk the Angel Falls Trail north 2 miles from Leatherwood Ford, you'll find there an impressive boulder rapids in the river, but no longer a waterfall.

ROCK SHELTERS

Overhangs of rock are surely the most numerous of the prominent geologic formations in the Big South Fork area. You usually cannot hike a trail without passing at least a small one, and there are many that are quite large.

Rock shelters form in vertical rock walls when softer layers of shale and sandstone below the Rockcastle Conglomerate are exposed. These less resistant layers erode more easily. The rock fractures and falls away, creating a cavity. Weathering that often includes seepage from the cavity causes more sections to collapse, enlarging the opening until the more resistant sandstone at the top is reached, which then forms the ceiling.

One of the best places for viewing rock shelters is along the Middle Creek Nature Trail. Take TN154 to Divide Road and turn east 0.7 mile to the Middle Creek Trailhead. You'll see several large rock shelters along this 3.2-mile loop. You can also take a connector off this trail to the Slave Falls Loop where you'll find the Indian Rock House, an especially

The Geology

Indian Rock House on the Slave Falls Loop

large rock shelter that was perhaps used by the Native Americans that once hunted the region. The archaeological resources and the presence of endangered plants and animals make the rock shelters sites of special concern for preservation. Do not camp, build fires, or dig in any rock shelter; they are protected by law.

You'll find an interesting rock shelter along the Dome Rockhouse Trail that you can access at the Station Camp East Trailhead on the Station Camp Road on the east side of the park. It's a 2.2-mile walk or horse ride along the trail to the rock shelter, which has an unusual domed ceiling.

The Biological Communities

The biology of the Big South Fork National River and Recreation Area is relatively diverse because the glaciers of the last ice age never reached this far south and so did not destroy ecosystems as they did to the north. This diversity of life gathers into several identifiable biological communities in the Big South Fork region. These distinct gatherings of plants and animals owe their segregation to differences in slope exposure, moisture, soil conditions, and isolation.

THE FORESTS

You can identify most of the forest communities of the Big South Fork as you descend from the rim of the gorge to the river's edge. Take a slow drive along TN297 down to Leatherwood Ford, either from the east or west. Or you can drive the Mine 18 Road down to the Blue Heron Community in the Kentucky portion of the park. If you prefer to walk, choose one of the trails that descend to the river, like the Leatherwood Ford Loop from the East Rim Trailhead, or the Twin Arches Trail and Loop from the Trailhead down to Charit Creek Lodge, or the Blue Heron Loop, which has an access on the Gorge Overlooks Road.

Heading across the surface of the plateau toward the river gorge, you'll observe open fields scattered among a second-growth forest. The trees were nearly all logged at one time for timber or simply to make way for agriculture, but in many places they have returned to create a deep woods.

This Uplands Forest consists primarily of mixed oak and Virginia pine. You may see white-tail deer browsing at the edge of the fields. Hawks and crows soar the currents. Hairy woodpeckers, northern flickers, and pileated woodpeckers search the trees for insects. The pine warbler and red-breasted nuthatch forage for conifer seeds. The seeds and acorns are food also for the red crossbill, evening grosbeak, bobwhite, turkey, gray squirrel, eastern chipmunk, and white-footed mouse. The eastern cottontail romps in and out of foliage near the ground.

Then as you reach the gorge and begin your descent, you'll see exposed blocks of sandstone at the rim. These upper walls of the gorge stand bare except for a few irregularities in the rock surface that provide footholds for alum root, a few ferns, and small shrubs and wind-swept pines. Vultures, eastern phoebes, and swallows nest in crevices in the cliff face. An occasional bat clings to the underside of an overhang or rock shelter. The red-tailed hawk surveys the gorge from a perch. If you are on foot, be careful of the timber rattlesnake and northern copperhead that might lie on a rock, basking in the bright sun.

From the base of the exposed rock walls, you'll see steep wooded slopes that drop toward the river. Much of this Ravine Forest was once logged, but it has revived and there still exist occasional coves of old-growth forest. The Ravine Forest consists of overlapping communities.

Exposed south-facing slopes possess mixed-oak and tulip poplar communities where turkey, gray squirrel, and opossum are attracted to the mast and thick undergrowth. The wood thrush, hooded warbler, and downy woodpecker frequent the understory of dogwood, maple, redbud, sourwood, holly, sassafras, and serviceberry. The red-eyed vireo, scarlet tanager, and tufted-titmouse feed in the canopy. In spring and early summer, you'll see the blooms of laurel and occasional azalea.

Look into the dark, shaded coves of the north-facing slopes. Where understory and groundcover are inhibited, hemlock and rhododendron live in virtual solitude except for a passing deer, bobcat, or fox. Kentucky and blackpole warblers and the golden-crowned kinglet search for seeds and insects in the canopy.

Descend farther to the lower slopes where the soil is deep, moist, and rich in nutrients. Here you'll find the mixed-mesophytic forest where

The Ravine Forest from the Grand Gap Loop

several hardwood species predominate. A forest of sugar maple, beech, poplar, basswood, ash, and buckeye harbor the gray fox, skunk, and raccoon. The barred owl and red-shouldered hawk search for the smoky shrew, eastern mole, eastern woodrat, golden mouse, and short-tail shrew.

After your winding descent, you'll level out along the floor of the gorge. Here you'll see an alluvial forest of sycamore and river birch with wild oats and dense stands of cane farther downstream; beaver, muskrat, and otter live in synchronization with the river. The Louisiana waterthrush, spotted sandpiper, and American woodcock explore the wet sand.

At the river's edge, notice a gravel and rubble zone possessing a few shrubs. The strip is inhabited by the bullfrog, southern leopard frog, pickerel frog, water snake, and midland painted turtle. Deer and other large species come to the stream for water as wood ducks paddle by.

Recent floods have perhaps left debris hanging in the limbs of shrubs and trees along the riverbank. Small pools deserted by the retreating waters and replenished by rains are filled with life in spring. Salamanders and turtles grope through the sedges, rushes, moss, and reeds of more permanent pools. Swallows and eastern bluebirds flit across the pools as they feed on the numerous insects attracted to the water. Puddles serve as nurseries for amphibians that hurry toward maturity.

Once you reach a parking area at the river, you might get out of your car and dangle your bare feet in the water. The river breathes with its rapids and riffles, giving life to the riverweed growing on the flooded rocks with diatoms and algae in association. These support the zooplankton and aquatic insects that are food for the bluebreast darter, walleye, longear sunfish, and smallmouth bass. Mussels with unusual names like mule ear, pink lady finger, and pistol grip cling to the submerged rocks. Belted kingfishers skim the surface, and green herons lunge for fish and amphibians.

Look back up the wooded slopes of the gorge. The different communities combine into one, and you'll see not distinct boundaries, but a wholeness and a balance reclaimed by nature.

PLANT IDENTIFICATION

To help in identifying trees in the area, you can walk the 2.0-mile Angel Falls Trail heading north from Leatherwood Ford. You can pick up a trail brochure at the information gazebo at Leatherwood Ford or at the Bandy Creek Visitor Center. Matching the brochure's identifications with numbered posts along the trail, you'll be introduced to 30 trees and shrubs of the Big South Fork Gorge. Numerous plant identification guides are available at bookstores and the Visitor Center.

In fall the forest trees present a show of color that's worth a visit to the park. The peak time is usually the middle to last of October. The drive down to Leatherwood Ford or to Blue Heron will give you a varied display. Any overlook in the park will present a sea of color, particularly the East Rim Overlook and the Bear Creek Overlook. For a short hike with good fall color, walk the 0.7-mile Twin Arches Trail from the Twin Arches Trailhead off Divide Road in the Middle Creek area of the park and climb the stairway to the top of the arches; if you're agile, you can then climb to the very top of South Arch for a full-circle vista.

Spring is the best time for viewing wildflowers, but you'll find blooming plants along trails and roads nearly anytime from March through October. Two of the best trails for seeing wildflowers are the John Muir Trail north and south from Leatherwood Ford as it passes along the river and the Angel Falls Trail north from Leatherwood Ford. The Honey Creek Loop near the Burnt Mill Bridge Access is also good for wildflowers where it follows the streams, but be aware this is a difficult hike. In Kentucky, you can walk the Blue Heron Loop south from the Blue Heron Mining Community toward Devil's Jump Rapids to see wildflowers. Actually, any trail along the river, where it is more moist, should have good wildflowers. Do not pick, dig, or collect wildflowers or any plants within the BSFNRRA.

For both wildflowers and fall color, weather conditions and topographic locations affect the display. For wildflowers, temperatures and rainfall plus slope exposure alter blooming times. For fall color, temperature and rainfall alter the peak color time and the quality of the color for any given year—drier weather causes the color to appear earlier, although with less brilliance; once the color arrives, it lasts longer if warm, sunny days alternate with cool nights.

The Biological Communities

WILDLIFE WATCHING

Catching glimpses of wildlife, whatever activity you are engaged in, rewards you with a sense of bonding with the natural world. In revealing itself to you, an animal accepts you into its world, if only for a fleeting moment.

Perhaps birding is the most popular type of wildlife watching. Birds in the Big South Fork are both migratory as well as resident. The resident birds are either permanent, winter, or summer. So if you want to see each type of bird that visits the park, you'll need to come at all seasons of the year. Bring your binoculars, a birding book, sturdy shoes, and a broad-brimmed hat for sunny days.

Wildlife watching can be an additional attraction to hiking and even road touring. Walking quietly on the trails, you may get to see turkey running across your path, wild pig scampering along a stream, squirrels, chipmunks, and rabbits rustling the leaves along your path, or grouse bursting from cover. From your car, traveling during the quiet mornings and cool evenings, you may see deer ambling in open fields, hawks

Birdwatching (Courtesy of the NPS)

Exploring the Big South Fork

soaring overhead, fox and raccoon dashing out of view. Along the river, whether walking or paddling, watch for ducks, fish, and water snakes; you might even see river otter and beaver.

Do not approach any wild animal; you will disrupt their natural activities, and the animal may see you as a threat and try to defend itself. Do not feed the animals, which will cause them to become dependent on humans for food. Simply watch from a distance, take a picture, and move on. If you are in a car, do not stop in the road; continue on to a parking area. At night, do not use car headlights or other lights, including flashlights, to spot animals; that is a tactic used by illegal hunters.

While you're in the park, protect wildlife habitat. Tread lightly—put turned-over rocks back in their natural position, leave alone standing dead trees which are used by wildlife for homes and food sources, carry out all trash.

Trees of the Big South Fork

CONIFERS	BROAD-LEAFED	
Northern White Cedar*	Alder	American Elm
Red Cedar	Green Ash	Red Elm
	White Ash	Winged Elm
Eastern Hemlock	Big Tooth Aspen	
		Fringetree
Pines	Basswood	
Eastern White Pine	American Beech	Hackberry
Pitch Pine	Yellow Birch	Hazelnut
Shortleaf Pine	River Birch	Hickories
Virginia Pine	Blackgum	Bitternut Hickory
	Boxelder	Mockernut Hickory
	Buckeye	Pignut Hickory
	Butternut*	Shagbark Hickory
		American Holly
	Chestnut	Hophornbeam
	Allegheny Chinquapin*	
	Cottonwood	Ironwood
	Swamp Dogwood	Black Locust
	Flowering Dogwood	

(Cont.)

Rare, threatened, endangered, or of special concern

The Biological Communities

Magnolias
  Bigleaf Magnolia
  Cucumber
    Magnolia
  Frazier Magnolia
  Umbrella Magnolia
Maples
  Red Maple
  Striped Maple
  Sugar Maple
Red Mulberry

Oaks
  Black Oak
  Blackjack Oak
  Chestnut Oak
  Northern Red Oak
  Post Oak
  Scarlet Oak
  Southern Red Oak
  White Oak

Pawpaw
Persimmon
Tulip Poplar

Redbud

Sassafras
Serviceberry
Sourwood
Sweetgum
Sycamore

Black Walnut
Black Willow
Silky Willow
Witchhazel

Fall Color at the Big South Fork

REDS

Dogwood
Red Maple
Northern Red Oak
Southern Red Oak
White Oak
Serviceberry

SCARLETS

Blackgum
Scarlet Oak
Sourwood
Sumac
Sweetgum

YELLOWS

Basswood
American Beech
River Birch
Yellow Birch
Buckeye
Cottonwood
Hickories
Hophornbeam
Striped maple
Red Mulberry
Chestnut Oak
Pawpaw
Persimmon
Poplar
Redbud
Black Walnut

RED-ORANGES

Sassafras
Sugar maple

Wildflowers of the Big South Fork

**EARLY SPRING
(March)**

Bloodroot
Early Saxifrage
Harbinger-of-Spring
Hepatica
Purple Cress
Purslane Speedwell
Rue Anemone
Spring Beauty
Star Chickweed
Trout Lily
Twinleaf

MID-SPRING (April)

Allegheny Spurge
Birdfoot Violet
Blue Cohosh
Blue Phlox
Bluets
Buttercups
Common Blue Violet
Common Cinquefoil
Crested Dwarf Iris
Cut-leaved Toothwort
Dwarf Larkspur
Dutchman's Breeches
Erect Trillium
Fire Pink
Foamflower
Golden Ragwort
Halberd-leaved Violet
Large-flowered
    Trillium
Little Brown Jug
Long-spurred Violet
Mercury Spurge*
Mountain Spurge
Pennywort
Pussy Toes

Slender Toothwort
Smooth Yellow Violet
Spiderwort
Spring Cress
Squirrel Corn
Stone Crop
Winter Cress
Yellow Trillium

LATE SPRING (May)

Appalachian
    Sandwort*
Bindweed
Canada Violet
Chickweed
Coreopsis
Cumberland
    Sandwort*
Dwarf Dandelion
Dwarf Ginseng*
False Solomon's-Seal
Green and Gold*
Indian Cucumber-
    Root
Indian Pink
Jack-in-the-Pulpit
Large-flowered
    Bellwort
Lyre-leaved Sage
May Apple
Mountain Laurel
Pink Lady's Slipper*
Queen Anne's Lace
Showy Orchis
Solomon's-Seal
Swamp White Violet
Sweet Cicely
Sweet White Violet
Trailing Arbutus
Violet Wood Sorrel
Virginia Bluebell

White Baneberry
White Violet
Wild Columbine
Wild Geranium
Wild Oats
Wild Sweet William
Wild Yam
Wood Nettle
Yellow Lady's Slipper*
Yellowroot

**EARLY SUMMER
(June)**

Alum-Root
Beard-Tongue
Black Cohosh
Blue-eyed Grass
Butterflyweed
Catawba
    Rhododendron
Common Milkweed
Common Skullcap
Daisy Fleabane
Evening Primrose
Flame Azalea
Goat's-Beard
Goat's-Rue
Hop Clover
Indian Pipe
Lamb's Quarters
Lizard's Tail
Meadow Parsnip
Orange Hawkweed
Ox-eye Daisy
Pipsissewa (Spotted
    Wintergreen)
Putty-Root
Ragwort
Rosebay
    Rhododendron
Rough Hawkweed*

(Cont.)

Rare, threatened, endangered, or of special concern

The Biological Communities

Ruellia	Smartweed	Rough-leaved
St. Johnswort	Spotted Joe-Pye-Weed	Sunflower
Teaberry (Wintergreen)	Spreading False	Small Sundrops*
Venus' Looking Glass	Foxglove*	Star Tickseed*
Viper's Bugloss	Tick Trefoil	Sweet Everlasting
Waterleaf	Virginia Dayflower	Thread-leaf Sundrops*
Whorled Loosestrife	White Avens	Tickseed
Wood-Sage	Wild Hydrangea	Turtlehead
Yellow Wood Sorrel	Wood Lily*	White Lettuce
		White-topped Aster
MID-SUMMER (July)	**LATE SUMMER**	Woodland Sunflower
	(August)	Yellow Leaf-Cup
Agrimony		
Bedstraw	Beggarticks	**AUTUMN**
Black-eyed Susan	Beebalm	**(September-October)**
Blue Ridge False	Bergamot	
Foxglove*	Blazing Star	Autumn Sneezeweed
Cardinal Flower	Blue Monkshood*	Calico Aster
Dodder	Common Thistle	Eastern Silvery Aster*
Enchanter's	Crane-fly Orchid	Frost-weed Aster
Nightshade	Crested Fringed	Gall-of-the-Earth
Flowering Spurge	Orchid*	Goldenrods
Fringed Loosestrife	False Foxglove	Heart-leaved Aster
Hoary Mountain Mint	Golden Aster	Lion's-Foot
Jewelweed	Great Blue Lobelia	Lucy Braun's White
Leatherleaf Meadow	Harebell	Snakeroot*
Rue*	Hog Peanut	Mistflower
Nodding Wild Onion	Horse-Balm	Purple Gerardia
Partridgeberry	Ironweed	Rockcastle Aster*
Rattlesnake Plantain	Jerusalem Artichoke	Sticky Goldenrod*
Rose Pink	Monkey Flower	White Snakeroot
Rosebud Orchis	New England Aster	White Wood Aster
Sensitive Brier		

*Rare, threatened, endangered, or of special concern

A Sampling of Other Seed Plants of the Big South Fork

Ageratum*
American Barberry**
American
 Water-Pennywort**
Arrow Arum
Arrow-Wood

Bachelor's Button*
Barren Strawberry
Bastard-Toadflax
Beakrush
Beech-Drops
Beggar Lice
Birthwort
Blue Haw
Boneset
Box Huckleberry
Buckthorn
Buffalo Nut
Bugbane
Bulrush
Bur-Reed
Burdock*
Buttonbush
Butternut**

Carolina Rose
Catbrier
Cattail
Chickory*
Climbing Hydrangea
Clovers
Cocklebur*
Columbo
Common Daisy*
Common Mullein *
Common Rush
Coral Honeysuckle*
Coralberry
Croton

Cumberland
 Rosemary**

Daffodil*
Dandelion *
Daylily *
Dame's Rocket*
Devil's Walking Stick
Dewberry
Dock*
Dog Fennel*
Duckweed*
Dutchman's Pipe

Elderberry
Elephant's Foot

False Indigo
False Nettle
Fetterbush
Fireweed
Five-Fingers
Fly Poison
Fringed Nutrush**
Frost Grape

Galingale
Golden Alexander
Golden Club**
Golden Seal**
Grasses
 Barley
 Beardgrass**
 Bent Grass
 Big Bluestem
 Bluegrass
 Bottlebrush Grass
 Brome Grass
 Broomsedge
 Cane

Crabgrass*
Cut Grass
Fescue
Goose Grass*
Hair Grass
Indiangrass
Little Bluestem
Manna Grass
Melic Grass
Needle Grass
Oat Grass
Orchard Grass*
Panic Grass
Rye Grass*
Sweet Vernal Grass*
Switchgrass
Timothy*
Velvet Grass*
Wild Rye Grass

Hairy Snoutbean**
Hardhack
Hawthorn
Hedge Hyssop**
Henbit*
Heronsbill*
Honewort
Honey Locust
Horseweed

Indian Hemp
Indian-Physic
Indian Plantain
Indian Strawberry*

Japanese Honeysuckle*
Jumpseed

Kidneyleaf
 Grass-of-Parnassus**

*Non-native
**Rare, threatened, endangered, or of special concern

(Cont.)

The Biological Communities

Kudzu*

Large-flowered
  Barbara's Buttons**
Leatherwood
Lespedeza
Leucothoe
Liverleaf
Lopseed
Lousewort
Lovage

Maleberry
Maple-leafed Viburnum
Mexican Tea*
Milkweed
Mimosa*
Mistletoe
Mock Orange**
Morning-Glory
Mountain Camellia
Mountain Witch-Alder**
Muscadine

Nannyberry
New Jersey Tea
Ninebark
Nuttall's Small
  Reedgrass**

Obedient Plant

Passion Flower
Path Rush
Pepper-Vine
Peppergrass*
Periwinkle*
Pigweed*
Pinweed
Pirate Bush**

Poison Hemlock*
Poison Ivy
Poke Weed
Pondweeds
Possum Haw
Purple Coneflower

Rabbit Foot Clover*
Ragweed*
Riverweeds
Round-leaf Bitter
  Cress**
Round-leaf
  Fameflower**

Sedges
  Cypress-swamp
    Sedge**
  Heavy Sedge**
  Hop Sedge
  Tussock Sedge**
Shortleaf
  Sneezeweed**
Southern Crabapple**
Southern Heartleaf**
Sparkleberry
Spicebush
Spikerush
Squaw Huckleberry
Squaw-Root
Strawberry Bush
Sumacs
  Fragrant Sumac
  Smooth Sumac
  Winged Sumac
Summer Grape
Swamp Honeysuckle
Swamp Rose
Sweet-Clover*
Sweet Pinesap**

Sweet-Shrub**

Teasle*
Tennessee
  Pondweed**
Thoroughwort
Threadfoot**
Three-seeded Mercury
Trumpet Creeper

Valerian
Verbena
Vetch
Virginia Creeper
Virginia Heartleaf**
Virginia Spiraea**
Virginia Willow

Wafer-ash
Wapato
Water Hemlock
Water Plantain
Water Willow
Waxweed
White-leaved Leather-
  Flower**
Whitlow-Grass
Wild Asparagus*
Wild Blackberry
Wild Chervil
Wild Lettuce
Wild Parsnip
Wild Plum
Wild Quinine
Wild Sensitive Plant
Windflower
Woodrush

Yarrow*
Yellow-eyed Grass

*Non-native
**Rare, threatened, endangered, or of special concern

Exploring the Big South Fork

Ferns and Related Plants of the Big South Fork

American Climbing
Fern
Blunt-lobed Woodsia
Bracken Fern
Broad Beechfern
Christmas Fern
Cinnamon Fern
Fancy Fern
Glade Fern
Goldie's Woodfern
Filmy Fern*
Hay-scented Fern
Marsh Fern
Marginal Shield Fern
Maidenhair Fern
New York Fern
Purple Cliffbrake

Resurrection Fern
Rock Cap Fern
Royal Fern
Sensitive Fern
Silvery Spleenwort
Southern Lady Fern
Spreading Bladder
Fern
Sweet Fern*
Wooly-lip Fern

Alabama Grapefern
Common Grapefern
Rattlesnake Fern
Southern
Adder's-Tongue
Southern Grapefern

Ebony Spleenwort
Maidenhair Spleenwort
Mountain Spleenwort
Walking Fern

Scouring Rush

Quillwort

Fir Clubmoss
Ground Cedar
Ground Pine
Rock Clubmoss
Running Pine
Shining Clubmoss

Meadow Spikemoss

Mammals of the Big South Fork

Bats
Big Brown Bat
Eastern Pipistrel
Eastern Small-footed
Bat*
Evening Bat
Gray Bat*
Hoary Bat
Keen's Bat
Indiana Bat*
Little Brown Bat
Northern Long-eared
Bat*
Rafinesque's
Big-eared Bat*
Red Bat
Silver-haired Bat
Southeastern Bat

Beaver
Black Bear*
Bobcat

Coyote
Eastern Chipmunk
Eastern Cottontail

White-tail Deer

Gray Fox
Red Fox

Mink
Eastern Mole
Hairy-tail Mole

Mice
Cotton Mouse
Deer Mouse
Eastern Harvest
Mouse
Golden Mouse
House Mouse
Meadow Jumping
Mouse
White-footed Mouse
Woodland Jumping
Mouse*
Muskrat

Virginia Opossum
River Otter*

Wild Pig

(Cont.)

Rare, threatened, endangered, or of special concern

The Biological Communities

Raccoon	Shrews	Meadow Vole
Rats	Least Shrew	
Black Rat	Masked Shrew	Long-tail Weasel
Hispid Cotton Rat	Short-tail Shrew	Woodchuck
Marsh Rice Rat	Smokey Shrew	
Eastern Woodrat*	Southeastern Shrew	
	Water Shrew	
Eastern Spotted Skunk*	Squirrels	
Striped Skunk	Fox Squirrel	
	Gray Squirrel	
	Southern Flying	
	Squirrel	

Resident and Migratory Birds of the Big South Fork

(not all species have been observed, but are likely to be present)

**PERMANENT
RESIDENT**

Great Blue Heron
Canada Goose
Mallard
Black Vulture*
Turkey Vulture
Sharp-shinned Hawk*
Cooper's Hawk*
Red-shouldered Hawk*
Red-tailed Hawk
American Kestrel
Ruffed Grouse
Wild Turkey
Northern Bobwhite
Killdeer
American Woodcock
Rock Dove
Mourning Dove
Common Barn Owl
Eastern Screech-Owl
Great Horned Owl

Barred Owl
Belted Kingfisher
Red-headed
   Woodpecker
Red-bellied
   Woodpecker
Downy Woodpecker
Hairy Woodpecker
Northern Flicker
Pileated Woodpecker
Eastern Phoebe
Horned Lark
Blue Jay
Common Crow
Carolina Chickadee
Tufted Titmouse
White-breasted
   Nuthatch
Carolina Wren
Eastern Bluebird
American Robin
Northern Mockingbird
Brown Thrasher

Cedar Waxwing
European
   Starling
Pine Warbler
Northern
   Cardinal
Rufous-sided
   Towhee
Field Sparrow
Song Sparrow
Red-winged
   Blackbird
Eastern
   Meadowlark
Common
   Grackle
Brown-headed
   Cowbird
Red Crossbill
American
   Goldfinch
House Sparrow

(Cont.)

Rare, threatened, endangered, or of special concern

Exploring the Big South Fork

SUMMER RESIDENT (Sp, Su, F)

Green-backed Heron
Black-crowned Night-Heron
Yellow-crowned Night-Heron
Wood Duck
Broad-winged Hawk
Black-billed Cuckoo
Yellow-billed Cuckoo
Common Nighthawk
Chuck-will's-widow
Whip-poor-will
Chimney Swift
Ruby-throated Hummingbird
Eastern Wood Pewee
Acadian Flycatcher
Willow Flycatcher
Eastern Kingbird
Purple Martin
Northern Rough-winged Swallow
Barn Swallow
House Wren
Blue-gray Gnatcatcher
Wood Thrush
Gray Catbird
White-eyed Vireo
Solitary Vireo
Yellow-throated Vireo
Red-eyed Vireo
Golden-winged Warbler
Northern Parula
Yellow Warbler
Chestnut-sided Warbler
Black-throated Green Warbler
Yellow-throated Warbler
Prairie Warbler

Cerulean Warbler
Black and White Warbler
American Redstart
Prothonotary Warbler
Worm-eating Warbler
Swainson's Warbler*
Ovenbird
Louisiana Waterthrush
Kentucky Warbler
Common Yellowthroat
Hooded Warbler
Yellow-breasted Chat
Summer Tanager
Scarlet Tanager
Indigo Bunting
Chipping Sparrow
Bachman's Sparrow *
Grasshopper Sparrow
Orchard Oriole

WINTER RESIDENT (F, W, Sp)

Common Loon
Pied-billed Grebe
Horned Grebe
Green-winged Teal
American Black Duck
Northern Pintail
Gadwall
American Widgeon
Canvasback
Redhead
Ring-necked Duck
Lesser Scaup
Common Goldeneye
Bufflehead
Hooded Merganser
Common Merganser
Red-breasted Merganser
Bald Eagle*

Golden Eagle*
American Coot
Common Snipe
Ring-billed Gull
Yellow-bellied Sapsucker
Red-breasted Nuthatch
Brown Creeper
Winter Wren
Golden-crowned Kinglet
Ruby-crowned Kinglet
Hermit Thrush
Yellow-rumped Warbler
Tree Sparrow
Savannah Sparrow
Fox Sparrow
Swamp Sparrow
White-throated Sparrow
White-crowned Sparrow
Dark-eyed Junco
Rusty Blackbird
Purple Finch
Pine Siskin
Evening Grosbeak

MIGRANT ONLY (Sp, F)

American Bittern
Blue-winged Teal
Osprey *
Northern Harrier
Peregrine Falcon*
Sandhill Crane
Greater Yellowlegs
Lesser Yellowlegs
Solitary Sandpiper
Spotted Sandpiper
Semipalmated Sandpiper
Least Sandpiper
Pectoral Sandpiper
Olive-sided Flycatcher
Least Flycatcher
Tree Swallow
Bank Swallow

(Cont.)

Rare, threatened, endangered, or of special concern

The Biological Communities

Cliff Swallow
Sedge Wren
Marsh Wren
Veery
Gray-cheeked Thrush
Swainson's Thrush
Warbling Vireo
Philadelphia Vireo
Blue-winged Warbler
Tennessee Warbler
Orange-crowned
  Warbler

Nashville Warbler
Magnolia Warbler
Cape May Warbler
Black-throated Blue
  Warbler
Blackburnian Warbler
Palm Warbler
Bay-breasted Warbler
Blackpoll Warbler
Northern Waterthrush

Connecticut Warbler
Mourning Warbler
Wilson's Warbler
Canada Warbler
Rose-breasted
  Grosbeak
Vesper Sparrow
Lincoln's Sparrow
Bobolink
Northern Oriole

Reptiles of the Big South Fork

Cumberland Turtle
Eastern Box Turtle
Eastern Mud Turtle
Eastern Spiny Softshell
Map Turtle
Midland Painted Turtle
Midland Smooth
  Softshell
Ouachita Map Turtle
Snapping Turtle
Stinkpot
Stripe-necked Musk
  Turtle

Eastern Slender Glass
  Lizard
Northern Fence Lizard
Six-lined Racerunner

Broad-headed Skink
Five-lined Skink
Ground Skink
Northern Coal Skink
Southeastern
  Five-lined Skink*

Black Kingsnake
Black Rat Snake
Eastern Earth Snake
Eastern Garter Snake
Eastern Hognose
  Snake
Eastern Milk Snake
Eastern Ribbon Snake
Eastern Worm Snake
Midland Brown Snake

Midwest Worm Snake
Northern Black Racer
Northern Copperhead
Northern Pine Snake
Northern Red-bellied
  Snake
Northern Ringneck
  Snake
Northern Scarlet Snake
Northern Water Snake
Queen Snake
Rough Green Snake
Scarlet Kingsnake
Southeastern Crowned
  Snake
Timber Rattlesnake

*Rare, threatened, endangered, or of special concern

Amphibians of the Big South Fork

Eastern Tiger Salamander	Northern Two-lined Salamander	Blanchard's Cricket Frog
Four-toed Salamander	Red-spotted Newt	Bullfrog
Green Salamander*	Seal Salamander	Gray Treefrog
Hellbender*	Slimy Salamander	Green Frog
Long-tailed Salamander	Small-mouthed Salamander	Mountain Chorus Frog
Marbled Salamander	Spotted Salamander	Pickerel Frog
Midland Mud Salamander	Zigzag Salamander	Southern Leopard Frog
Mudpuppy	American Toad	Spring Peeper
Northern Dusky Salamander	Eastern Narrow-mouthed Toad	Upland Chorus Frog
Northern Red Salamander	Eastern Spadefoot	Wood Frog
Northern Spring Salamander	Fowler's Toad	

Fish of the Big South Fork

GAME SPECIES | | **NON-GAME SPECIES**

Brook Trout	Channel Catfish	Bigeye Chub
Brown Trout	Flathead Catfish	Black Redhorse
Rainbow Trout	Yellow Bullhead	Brook Silverside
		Buffalo
Bluegill	Ohio Muskellunge	Carp
Crappie	Sauger	Creek Chub
Green Sunfish	Walleye	Drum
Longear Sunfish		Gar
		Golden Redhorse
Coosa Bass		Log Perch
Kentucky Bass		Northern Hog Sucker
Largemouth Bass		Northern Redhorse
Rock Bass		Paddlefish
Smallmouth Bass		Quillback Carpsucker
Spotted Bass		Shovelnose Sturgeon
Striped Bass/Rockfish		Slender Madtom
White Bass		Stonecat
		Stoneroller
		Warmouth
		White Sucker (Cont.)

Rare, threatened, endangered, or of special concern

The Biological Communities

Blacknose Dace	Spotfin Shiner	Channel Darter
Common Shiner	Telescope Shiner	Dusky Darter
Emerald Shiner	Tennessee Shiner	Duskytail Darter*
Mimic Shiner	Whitetail Shiner	Emerald Darter
Rosefin Shiner		Greenside Darter
Rosyface Shiner*	Arrow Darter	Olive Darter*
Rosyside Dace	Ashy Darter*	Rainbow Darter
Sand Shiner	Banded Darter	Speckled Darter
Sawfin Shiner*	Barcheek Darter	Spotted Darter
Southern Redbelly	Blackside Darter	Stripetail Darter
Dace	Bluebreast Darter	Tippecanoe Darter*

Mussels and Crustaceans of the Big South Fork

Cumberland Bean	Little-wing Pearly	Pocketbook
Pearly Mussel*	Mussel*	Tan Riffleshell*
Cumberland Elktoe*	Mucket	Tennessee Clubshell*
Cumberlandian	Mule Ear	White Wartyback
Combshell*	Oyster Mussel*	
Fluted Kidneyshell*	Pink Lady-Finger	Big South Fork
Kidneyshell	Pistol Grip	Crayfish*
Heelsplitter		

Rare, threatened, endangered, or of special concern

The People of the Big South Fork

W hen you visit the BSFNRRA, you'll see a virtual wilderness that you might think people have seldom visited. But the park area has often contained the habitations and accouterments of humans, from Indian camps to lumber and mining camps, from wagon roads to rail lines, from coal mines to oil and gas wells. What you'll see upon visiting the park is a wilderness being reclaimed—second-growth forests cover the land, old roads melt into the landscape, man-made structures succumb to time. Yet the story of the people of the Big South Fork is preserved in the dust of rock shelters, in a few remaining cabins and buildings, in the cemeteries scattered within the boundaries, in historic exhibits, and in the memories of the people.

EARLY IMMIGRANTS

The first people to visit the Big South Fork region we now call "Native Americans"; they were here when the first white men came. But they too were immigrants, having come from the Old World to the New across the Bering Strait. They infiltrated North America in several waves of migration and cultural assimilation, from the Paleo-Indians, through the Archaic and Woodland cultures, to the Mississippian tradition.

Originally they were big game hunters. Later they developed pottery and began harvesting nuts and berries and gathering shellfish and walleye from the river. By 1000 AD, they had become farmers, growing much of their food; squash and corn were their primary diet, always supplemented with game they killed. But with a turn to agriculture, the people eventually left the highlands for the fertile and broad river valleys that were more suitable for growing crops.

When white men entered the southeast region, the people had coalesced into the historic tribes—the Cherokees, Chickasaws, Creeks, and Shawnees among them. The Cherokees and Shawnees dominated the Cumberland Plateau region, the Shawnees to the north and the Cherokees to the south. Both tribes, along with the lesser tribes, used the plateau as a hunting ground, often camping under the rock shelters found nearly everywhere.

Indian trails crossed the Big South Fork region. Most prominent was the Great Tellico Trail running north to south along a ridge east of the Big South Fork; US27 generally follows the route of this ancient Indian trail that once connected the Cumberland River with Sequatchie Valley to the south. One of the east-west trails that intersected with the Great Tellico Trail later became the Huntsville-Monticello Road that forded the river at Big Island near the mouth of No Business Creek; this road is no longer open to vehicles. A branch of that road crossed the river at the mouth of Station Camp Creek.

Besides these pathways later used by white settlers, little remains of the presence of these people because they seldom lived in the area. Yet, archaeological work has turned up relics in the sandy floors of the rock shelters—evidence of campfires, arrowheads, pottery and stone utensils. By the time the park was created, much of the region had been picked over by amateur collectors, which destroyed much of the historical record. Today, relic collecting is prohibited by federal law in order to preserve the historical context of these remains. Each piece is the property now of the American public and should not be taken from its place.

Although you can no longer collect artifacts from the rock shelters, take a moment to stop on a hike that passes such an overhang. Imagine the people that once camped there. Here is a central place where they might have located their campfire. Over there is a dry spot where they could lie down for the night. Would they have been afraid of the gathering dark? Or would they have felt at home in the natural world that supplied their needs?

THE SETTLERS

The white men who first entered the region also used the rock shelters that had given refuge to the Indians. The long hunters of the Daniel Boone era surely camped under these overhangs to get out of the rain and stay warm around their campfires; they were called "long hunters" because they stayed out in the wilderness for a long time. Hunters lead by Kaspar Mansker in 1769 are thought to be the first white men to enter the Big South Fork country.

Treaties with the Cherokee Indians opened the Big South Fork region to settlement. New immigrants came from Virginia and North Carolina that were mostly of English and Scotch-Irish ancestry. They also at first stayed in the rock shelters, closing them off with leaning poles, until they had time to build better accommodations. They usually chose those that faced east and south so as to catch the warming rays of the sun.

From the rock shelters, these pioneers moved into pole huts with mud floors. Later they built log cabins with split-log flooring, a loft or second story, and a stone chimney. The people cleared the land for crops and livestock and hunted for wild game, settling primarily along the creek and river valleys where the land was more fertile. These were a hardy and independent people who took pride in their own ingenuity and self-sufficiency.

As more people entered the region and families grew, communities formed around kinship lines; some of the first families were the Slavens, the Blevinses, and the Troxels. Each settlement generally occupied a particular watershed because communication and contact was much easier up and down a valley than over the steep ridge into the next valley. The larger settlements lay along the larger tributaries of the Big South Fork—Laurel Crossing Branch, Rock Creek, and Bear Creek in Kentucky and Williams, Station Camp, Parch Corn, and No Business Creeks in Tennessee. No Business Creek got its name, as one story goes, when a lone couple first tried to settle the region with the wife

The People of the Big South Fork

saying they had no business leaving home and no business trying to stay there.

These settlements remained isolated for much of the 1800s, except for the Civil War period when many men from the region left to fight, most with the Union Army. Kentucky remained with the Union, and while Tennessee joined the Confederacy, this northeast region remained sympathetic with the Union. Those remaining at home were subjected to raiding parties, mostly posing as Confederates, but there were occasionally raiders that aligned themselves with the Union side as well. The raiding parties took food and livestock and often killed civilians. A Home Guard was established to protect the people from these raiders. After the Civil War, the communities turned inward again.

Much later, changing lifestyles that accompanied industrial development and the arrival of the automobile encouraged more recent generations to relocate near main roads in such settlements as Black Oak, White Pine, and Alticrest that developed along the Leatherwood Ford Road.

You can see a few of the old farmsteads that still remain from these older and newer settlements, with a little walking. Start with the 0.8-mile trail that leads down to Charit Creek Lodge. In the Middle Creek area, take Fork Ridge Road east off Divide Road; after passing the Sawmill Trailhead, keep left at a fork and drive 3.5 miles to parking for the trailhead. A road continues on down to the lodge, but it's gated to prevent vehicle access. The trail starts at the upper end of the parking area; horse riders and mountain bikers can take the road down. At the end of the trails, Charit Creek Lodge sits at the confluence of Charit Creek with Station Camp Creek. The lodge with additional log cabins provides backcountry accommodations; you'll need to make reservations prior to going if you want to spend the night.

The main lodge structure at Charit Creek incorporates an old log cabin some say was the homeplace of Jonathan Blevins, one of the earliest settlers of the region. Born in Virginia in 1779, he first moved with his parents to North Carolina before they made a final move to Kentucky in the late 1700s. According to the Blevins family genealogy study, Jonathan Blevins settled in the Bell Farm area along Rock Creek to the

Charit Creek Lodge

northwest of the park and then moved into the Scott County area of Tennessee sometime between 1850 and 1860. Some say he first settled on No Business Creek, but for sure he ended up living on Station Camp Creek, perhaps at the site of the lodge, but also perhaps farther down the creek near where he is buried.

The original log cabin that is now part of Charit Creek Lodge was erected sometime before Jonathan Blevins arrived, probably around 1816; it's not known by whom. The oldest part of the house is the one-room log cabin with chimney that's the far west part of the lodge. Another room was added later, almost as a separate cabin but with the chimney in the middle connecting the two, creating what's called a "saddlebag" cabin. The comparatively rough-hewn logs of the addition may indicate that different people built the two portions of the cabin.

In 1803, Blevins had married Katy Troxel, the daughter of Jacob Troxel and Cornblossom, the daughter of the Cherokee Chief

Chuqualatague, or "Doublehead." Troxel had been sent into the region during the American Revolution to befriend the Cherokees and thus help ensure they did not side with the British. He was called "Big Jake" because he stood over six feet tall. After becoming enamored with the chief's daughter, he married her and stayed in the region until his death in 1810. An official U.S. Army headstone erected at the KY700 turnoff to the Yahoo Falls Scenic Area marks the general location where some of his descendents think he was buried. Other accounts say he left the region and died later in Alabama.

Katy Troxel died in 1813 or 1814. When Jonathan Blevins brought his family that may have still included several children to Station Camp, he was married to Sarah Minton. Blevins died in 1863 from bee stings and is buried in the Hatfield Cemetery about two miles below the lodge on Station Camp Creek.

Later, others lived at Charit Creek—Jonathan Burke and William Riley Hatfield, both of whom lie in a small cemetery above the lodge

John Blevins Barn at Charit Creek Lodge (Courtesy of Audney Lloyd)

Exploring the Big South Fork

stables. Later, John Blevins, a great grandson of Jonathan Blevins lived there. Around 1930, he and his son, Oscar, built the four-crib barn of hand-hewn hemlock and oak logs that's located near the lodge; they followed the design of the original barn that had burned. John Blevins, again probably with Oscar, also built the hand-hewn log corncrib that stands in front of the lodge and the rived-log blacksmith shop behind the lodge. The last family to live there, the Phillips, sold the homesite to Joe Simpson around 1963, who operated it as the Parch Corn Hunting Lodge until 1982, when the U.S. Army Corps of Engineers purchased it for the park. Simpson brought in logs from other houses in the area to create the two smaller cabins that now serve as bunkhouses. One was the Jacob Blevins, Jr. cabin from up Station Camp Creek and the other was the Appalonia Slaven cabin from farther down creek, also called the "Ellen Place" for the wife of Daniel Blevins; they were early residents. Logs from a house Simpson found in Slagle Hollow, Kentucky, now make up the east end of the main lodge building. A newer barn to the east side of the complex that was erected by Simpson now serves as the horse stables.

After the complex became part of the BSFNRRA, it was renamed "Charit Creek," after the creek that flows beside it. At first it operated as a youth hostel, but it then became a lodge for the general public.

Station Camp Creek, which flows in front of the lodge, was so named because it was first a gathering place for early long hunters, or some say a place where militia took station. The camp was probably established by men from the Watauga Settlement, one of the earliest settlements in what was to become the state of Tennessee.

The long hunters and their descendents settled the valley along the creek so that by 1850 there were 126 people living on subsistence farms in the valley. In the 1930s, Station Camp still had a post office. Nothing of the community remains now except a few small cemeteries and the old cabin and outbuildings at Charit Creek Lodge.

It's the far bunkhouse cabin within the lodge complex that was built with logs from the Jacob Blevins, Jr. homeplace. You can get to Jake's Place by walking the Twin Arches/Charit Creek Loop clockwise from Charit Creek 1.4 miles. The homesite may date to about the same time

Jacob Blevins, Jr. (Courtesy of Audney Lloyd)

that the old cabin at Charit Creek Lodge was built. But it was in 1884 that Jacob Blevins, Jr., brought his new wife, Viannah West, here to a log cabin he built in the early 1880s. A grandson of Jonathan Blevins and Katy Troxel, Jacob Jr. was known as "Jakey" and as "Uncle Jake" in later years. He and his wife raised nine children at their homestead, including the John Blevins who later lived at the Charit Creek Lodge site. Jakey died in 1935, followed a decade later by Vie. Jake's Place was marked by a solitary stone chimney that has been dismantled; you'll just find there now a line of rocks where it fell, a forlorn place.

To continue the history of the Blevins family, you'll need to walk the Oscar Blevins Farm Loop. You can pick up a pamphlet guide to the trail at the Bandy Creek Visitor Center and then make your way to the Bandy Creek Trailhead, which is just west of the Visitor Center. About halfway along the 3.6-mile loop, you'll reach the Oscar Blevins Farm. An open field spreads out from a large barn flanked by a log house and outbuildings that include a corncrib; to the front stands a more modern frame house. The farm, a historic site representative of early 20th century homesteads in the region, was the home of Oscar and Martha Ermon Blevins; Oscar was a great-great grandson of Jonathan Blevins.

After growing up on Station Camp Creek, Oscar Blevins moved to this location with his new wife, Ermon, in 1940; they later had a son, Lawrence. They first lived in the older log house to the rear that had been built in the 1879 by John B. Blevins, Oscar's great uncle and a brother to Jacob Blevins, Jr. For the two-room, story and a half structure, hewn logs were used to construct the east room and sawn timbers were used for the west room, which was probably a later addition. The corncrib is another older structure, built of hewn logs around the same time as the log house.

Oscar and Ermon later built the more modern house that's part of the farmstead in a style typical of the region called the "Cumberland House." The characteristic layout is one and a half stories, two rooms wide and one or two rooms deep, two front doors with a long front porch, and perhaps a later addition. Such houses usually have a central chimney; the Blevins house, though, has two chimneys. The Blevins house is three rooms across, but still has the characteristic two front

The People of the Big South Fork

Chimney of Jake's Place before dismantling

Top: John B. Blevins Log House at Oscar Blevins Farm Site (Courtesy of Benita J. Howell)
Bottom: Oscar and Ermon Blevins Cumberland House (Courtesy of Audney Lloyd)

doors. The Cumberland House is wood frame construction, typically clapboard or covered with rolled asphalt. The design of the Cumberland House could have simply been a variation on the saddlebag log cabin, an improvement that occurred once different building materials became available. But it may be that the design was introduced to the region; the Cumberland House was among the types of houses found in coal camps around 1900.

The Blevinses moved into their new Cumberland House in 1950. The smokehouse behind the home was also built around 1950. Oscar Blevins built the large barn to the rear in 1963. In that more modern age, the Blevinses chose to continue to live a subsistence life-style as their ancestors had, independent and self-sufficient.

Oscar and Ermon Blevins still lived on their farm at the time the national river and recreation area was formed. They moved from their house to make way for the public park. They settled on Peters Ford Road to the south in 1979; Oscar died in 1988.

You can also see the Oscar Blevins Farm by continuing along the Bandy Creek Road another 2.4 miles beyond the Bandy Creek Trailhead; the road becomes gravel. A short gravel road to the left leads down to the farm.

Along the main road, before reaching the turn down to the Oscar Blevins farm site, you'll pass the Clara Sue Blevins Historic Site. Clara Sue Blevins (later Campbell) lived in a trailer parked on the site and owned the property at the time it was purchased for the park. You'll find there the Lora Blevins House, a story and a half, two-room log house built in 1927 by Lora E. Blevins, the father-in-law of Clara Sue. Blevins and his wife Tealie Slavy raised several children there; he had come from the Station Camp East area and she from No Business Creek. Their son, Leonard, married Clara Sue. These were a different line of Blevinses from Oscar Blevins' side of the family.

Although sawmill lumber was available at the time, Lora Blevins chose to build a log house, probably because it was inexpensive; he used trees on his own property, which were relatively small since most larger trees by then had already been cut down. The original porches and a shed addition to the house are missing, and an original stone chimney was replaced with the existing concrete-block chimney around

Lora E. Blevins House at Clara Sue Blevins Site (Courtesy of Bonita J. Howell)

1967. The site also has a story and a half, double-crib barn of partially hewn logs completed by Lora Blevins in the 1930s. You'll also see a single-pen log corncrib with a frame porch added along the front and a vertical plank shed added to one side, built about the same time. Next to the house stands a small well house with the well casing still protruding from the ground. A smokehouse that stood on the other side of the main house is now gone.

Adjacent to the Clara Sue Blevins Site, lies the Katie Blevins Cemetery where you can wander through the gravesites of some of the early settlers. Both Jacob, Jr. and Vie Blevins are buried there. Jakey's father, Jacob Blevins, the son of Jonathan and Katy Troxel and named for his grandfather, Jacob Troxel, was the first to be buried in the cemetery along with his wife Catherine, who was known as "Katie" or "Katy."

Oscar Blevins is buried here too, along with his father, John, and his mother, Louisa. Also look for the grave of Calvin Blevins, the brother of Oscar Blevins. Notice a different name at the foot of the grave. Local people tell the story of how one night Calvin killed a man with a shot meant to scare a group away from fish traps that Blevins and some

Katie Blevins Cemetery

friends had placed in the river. One side of the story says the shot glanced off a tree and into one of the men. To avoid possible retribution from the man's family and perhaps being forced into having to defend himself, and also perhaps afraid of what the law would think, Blevins left the area and joined the army under the name of John R. Phillips. Years later, he returned to the region to live out his days, maintaining his false name, although most people knew who he was. When he died in 1984, the U.S. Army honored his service with the plaque that bears the Phillips name, while his family laid the stone that bears his real name.

Exploring the Katie Blevins Cemetery, you'll find the graves of other Blevinses and those of the Slavens who were another prominent family. Some of the gravestones have the pictures of those buried. You can see Viannah Blevins, but Jakey's picture is gone. You can see on gravestones the likenesses of John and Elvira Litton, members of another of the Big South Fork families. The Litton home also lies near the Bandy Creek area. You can get to the John Litton Farm by walking a 5.9-mile loop. You can reach the loop by a connector trail from the Bandy Creek Trailhead, or you can drive into the campground and park near the swimming pool to access the trail. The farm is about halfway along the loop.

John Litton

The farmstead sits in a cove with the log cabin John Litton built around 1900 commanding the valley. Below the house you'll find an earthen dam holding a stream-fed pond still alive with fish. Above are rockhouses once enclosed with wooden rails where the family kept livestock. Sitting in the meadow, an English-style barn has a first story built of hewn logs and second of oak plank walls; its drivethrough is located on the side instead of the gable end. Built by Litton around 1900, the barn may have been assembled from more than one original building. The Littons raised several children here. John Litton died in 1935 and his wife, Vi, in 1945.

The Litton Farm is also referred to as the "General Slaven Farm." "General" was his name, not a military title. The Slavens were the only other family to live here; they added to the original cabin a wrap-around frame addition on the west and south sides and a porch on the north and east sides.

John Litton Farm

John Litton Cabin on Parch Corn Creek (Courtesy of Audney Lloyd)

John Litton was known as a master cabin builder and built several in the park, including the John Litton Cabin on Parch Corn Creek in 1881. The cabin is a story and a half, single pen, log house. You can reach the cabin area by hiking the John Muir Trail north into the backcountry from Leatherwood Ford or taking the horse trail north from Station Camp Creek. Continuing on these trails north of Parch Corn Creek, you'll enter the site of the old community around No Business Creek where about 125 people once lived. It was a community similar to that at Station Camp Creek to the south. You'll only find there now a few building and house foundations, chimney bases, and a lone intact chimney.

By the time the national river and recreation area was authorized in 1974, there were only about forty households of year-round residents still living within the proposed boundaries. Their lands were purchased for the establishment of the park.

The People of the Big South Fork

CEMETERIES

Perhaps the most numerous reminders of the pioneers and farmers that once settled the Big South Fork are their cemeteries. There are now 54 cemeteries or grave sites known within the BSFNRRA. Hiking or riding the backcountry, you'll occasionally come upon single grave sites or a gathering of a few headstones. If you find one of these while exploring the backcountry, you might note any inscriptions that are legible on the headstones and make note of the location and report to the rangers to make sure the site is one that is already known.

In addition, there are a number of larger cemetery plots where small communities once flourished. Many of these are maintained by descendents who still live in the area. If you're interested in the history of the region, it's fun to study the gravestones, tracing the lineage of the Big South Fork families, among them the Blevinses, the Slavens, the Troxels, the Phillips, the Waters, the Roysdens, the Watsons, the

Cemeteries and gravesites lie within the park boundaries

Spradlins, the Kings, the Dolens, the Boyatts, and the Ledbetters. For information on family histories and gravesites, you might contact the local county historical societies.

When the first of the pioneers who came to the area died, they were buried by their peers in a style consistent with 18th-century European burials; a grave was often covered with a coffin-shaped monolith or at times an arched stone crypt, which might be slabs of stone leaning against each other to form a roof over the grave. These capstones or crypts usually had the name of the deceased and date of birth and death inscribed.

Later generations seem to have lost this attachment to European burial traditions and so later graves are marked simply with inscribed head and foot stones of hand-hewn sandstone or limestone. With time and in the isolation of the Big South Fork country, there was a deterioration of literacy and so grammatical and spelling errors and reversed letters began to appear in the inscriptions. Some simply had the initials of the deceased and the dates of birth and death. From 1900 to the late 1920s, illiteracy was common, and gravestone inscriptions virtually disappeared; many graves were marked by unshaped fieldstones rather than shaped head stones.

When the coal and timber industries came to the region, education was brought back to the Big South Fork. So graves from the late 1920s and early 1930s possess gravestones with inscriptions that show an increase in literacy. In later years, inscribed gravestones of sandstone, limestone, concrete, and imported marble came to resemble the cultural norm for the wider region.

You might find at a few cemeteries a form of roofed protection for a grave; called a "grave house," it usually consists of a roof on posts over the gravesite. Many of the cemeteries also have benches to one side for graveside and memorial services.

The Park Service maintains access to cemeteries for those who have family buried within the boundaries of the BSFNRRA. Within the adjacent area, cemeteries can be reached with existing roads and possibly with improved levels of access in the future. Access to cemeteries in the gorge area will be limited to existing roads and trails

The People of the Big South Fork

Some Cemeteries at the Big South Fork

Cemetery	Directions
1 Katie Blevins Cemetery	At the Clara Sue Blevins Historic Site; take the Bandy Creek Road west 0.8 mile from the Visitor Center.
2 Hattie Blevins Cemetery	In the Middle Creek area; take the left fork off Divide Road at Three Forks 4.6 miles from TN154.
3 Terry Cemetery	In the Middle Creek area; take the right fork at Three Forks 0.2 mile beyond the turnoff for the Hattie Blevins Cemetery; this 5-mile road may be rough, so use 4-wheel drive, horses, or mountain bikes; the road is scheduled for improvement.
4 Dirt Rockhouse Cemetery	In the Middle Creek area; stay left on Fork Ridge Road, after the Sawmill Trailhead 1.1 miles from Divide Road, and then in 0.2 mile take the first road left into the cemetery.
5 Charit Creek Cemetery	Above the stables at Charit Creek Lodge; take Fork Ridge Road all the way to the parking area 3.5 miles beyond the Sawmill Trailhead and hike (0.8 mile) or ride horses or mountain bikes (1.5 miles) down to the lodge.
6 Hatfield Cemetery	Along Station Camp Creek; follow the Station Camp Creek Trail from the Charit Creek Lodge about 2 miles east.
7 Owens Cemetery	Along Station Camp Creek; follow the Station Camp Creek Trail another half mile east from the Hatfield Cemetery.
8 Slaven Cemetery	Near Chimney Rocks; take Station Camp Road from TN297 7.0 miles and turn left just beyond Chimney Rocks to the cemetery.

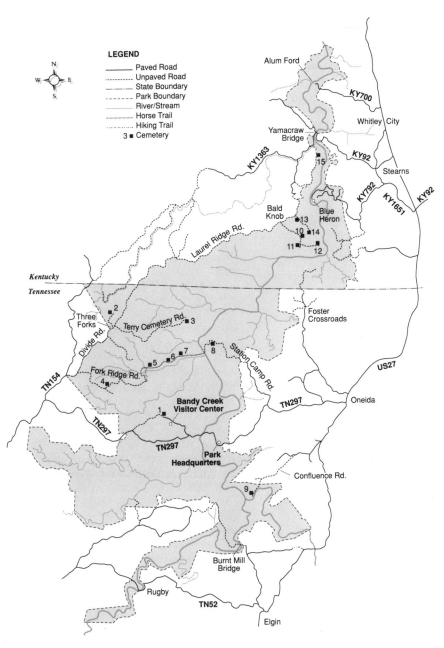

LEGEND

—————— Paved Road
·············· Unpaved Road
—··—··— State Boundary
— — — — Park Boundary
················· River/Stream
················· Horse Trail
············· Hiking Trail
3 ■ Cemetery

Alum Ford

KY700

Whitley City

Yamacraw
Bridge

KY1363

KY92

■15

Stearns

KY792

KY1651

KY92

Bald
Knob

Blue
Heron

■13

10■ ■14

11■

12

Laurel Ridge Rd.

Kentucky

Tennessee

Foster
Crossroads

Three
Forks

■2

Terry Cemetery Rd. ■3

Divide Rd.

■6 ■7

■5

■8

Station Camp Rd.

US27

Fork Ridge Rd.

4■

TN154

Bandy Creek
Visitor Center

1■

TN297

Oneida

TN297

TN297

Park
Headquarters

Confluence Rd.

9■

Burnt Mill
Bridge

Rugby

TN52

Elgin

Cemeteries within the BSFNRRA

The People of the Big South Fork

9 Phillips Cemetery	On the right, just before parking at the end of Confluence Road; south of Oneida on US27, follow the directions given in the section on paddling to the road that leads to the confluence behind the airport.
10 King Cemetery	Near the Ledbetter Place Trailhead; 4.9 miles along Beech Grove Road from KY1363, take Bald Knob Road south to the trailhead to park and then walk back up the road to where the KY Trail heads northeast off the road; follow the trail 0.2 mile up to the cemetery.
11 Hill Cemetery	Near the Ledbetter Place Trailhead; from the trailhead, continue down the Bald Knob road 0.2 mile to where an old road leads right with the cemetery just up this side road on your right.
12 Newt King Cemetery	At the end of Bald Knob Road; continue down the road from the Hill Cemetery turnoff 0.9 mile to end of road and cemetery up to left; this road has been improved but could still have a mud puddle or two after a rain and there's a steep section with loose gravel toward the end.
13 Barr Cemetery	Near Beech Grove Church; turn east off Beech Grove Road on the Waters Cemetery Road just west of Beech Grove Church or a half mile before the Bald Knob Road; this road is also used as a horse trail; you'll find the cemetery on the right in 0.3 mile where the horse trail turns off the road to the left.
14 Waters Cemetery	Near Beech Grove Church; continue down the Waters Cemetery Road from the Barr Cemetery to the road's end and the cemetery in one mile; although this road has been improved, there could be a mud puddle or two after a rain.

15 Wilson Cemetery

Before the Beech Grove community; 1.4 miles from KY1363 on the way to Beech Grove and Bald Knob, turn left on the graveled Wilson Ridge Road (there's also a dirt road to the left, but stay with the main gravel road); at 2.9 miles from the beginning of Wilson Ridge Road turn right up a small gravel road to the cemetery; on the way to the Wilson Cemetery, at 0.7 mile from the beginning of Wilson Ridge Road, you'll pass the large Nancy Graves Cemetery that's outside the park boundary.

maintained at the same level as when the land was turned over to the Park Service. You can at any time hike a trail into the gorge to visit a cemetery. But if you have family in a gorge cemetery and wish to visit using an existing road that is now closed to vehicular traffic, you may arrange to use the road by contacting the Chief Ranger at the park headquarters.

INDUSTRIAL DEVELOPMENT

The era of the pioneer settlements and subsistence farms lasted from the time Jonathan Blevins entered the region until his descendent Oscar Blevins and his wife Ermon moved away from their Big South Fork homestead to make way for the park. During this period, a new era of resource extraction began and then ran simultaneously with the farming communities.

The extractive industry started around 1812, when mining for saltpeter in the rock shelters of the Big South Fork helped to supply an essential ingredient for gun powder used in the War of 1812. Potassium nitrate, the chemical name of saltpeter, is found in the sandstone cliffs and rock walls and the floors of rock shelters. The saltpeter results from the decay of vegetation which releases nitrates that then leach down through the rock to collect at impermeable layers or soak into the soil of the shelter floors. The miners would blast rock from the walls and collect debris and soil from the rock shelters and put it all in large vats. They then poured boiling water over the rock and soil to dissolve the potassium

The People of the Big South Fork

nitrate. With filtering and boiling of the liquid that drained from the bottom of the vats, the miners had saltpeter crystals.

The commercial phase of the extractive industry perhaps began with the discovery of oil in 1818, although oil was not the objective.

In 1817, Marcus Huling and Andrew Zimmerman searched the Big South Fork country for a site to drill for salt, much sought after for use as a preservative in a time before refrigeration. They settled on a tract of land on the west side of the Big South Fork in Kentucky that they leased from Martin Beaty, who had recently purchased the land with the hope of beginning salt production.

After drilling to a depth of over 200 feet using a spring-pole rig they operated with their feet, Huling and Zimmerman struck oil rather than the salt-laden water they had hoped for. Unfortunately for the men, oil at the time was virtually worthless. Zimmerman gave up on the operation and left the area, but Huling remained, determined to make back his investment. He first tried to get his oil out of the wilderness by hiring some men to take a dugout canoe down river with a couple of barrels of oil lashed to it. The canoe wrecked at the Devil's Jump Rapids downstream, and the casks were thrown against boulders and burst open. That is perhaps how the rapids got its name; the locals called the oil "Devil's Tar" and said the Devil had jumped on the canoe to reclaim his property at the rapids. Another source of the name could have come from the men who later rode rafts of logs down river as a way of getting timber out of the river gorge; because of the danger of riding the rafts, the men were called "devils," and they would jump from their rafts when they approached this particularly difficult rapid.

After the failure of river transport for the oil, Huling managed to haul casks of the oil out of the gorge using a pack train of mules. He sold the oil to the makers of patent medicine in the United States and shipped at least 2000 gallons to Europe for use in liniments and other cure-alls. By 1820, Huling had given up the oil business because of the difficulty of transporting the oil to market and went back to drilling for salt in other places in the region. Yet, because some of the oil was actually sold, the Beaty Well, typically named for the landowner, qualifies as the first documented commercial oil well in the U.S. Although there had been similar oil strikes at other drillings for salt, there is no documentation to show that any of the oil was sold from those earlier wells.

You can visit the site of the Beaty Well, with a little difficulty. Although you'll only see a pipe sticking out of the ground, you can have a little adventure finding it. From the Yamacraw Bridge crossing of the Big South Fork on KY92, on the west side of the river, turn south on KY1363. At 2.3 miles, turn left on a gravel road that crosses Rock Creek on a concrete bridge; you'll see a sign for Bald Knob and Wilson Ridge. The road soon becomes paved once more. You'll pass through the community of Beech Grove, and then the road becomes gravel again at 4.7 miles. After ascending steeply, you'll reach Bald Knob and the Bald Knob Road to the left at 7.2 miles; turn left. This road has been improved to give access to a cemetery at its end, but it can still get muddy in places after a rain. At 1.4 miles down Bald Knob Road, you'll find parking for the Ledbetter Place Trailhead. You must then continue down the road, walking, for another 0.6 mile to a trail turnoff on the right; you could drive to here, but there's not much room for parking, maybe one car beside the road. Blazed with a red arrow, the trail, part of the Kentucky Trail, descends southeast along an old roadway that can get quite overgrown in summer. At about 1.7 miles, the trail crosses Oil Well Branch on a footbridge and then parallels the river where in about 500 feet the old well is off to your left between the trail and the river. The park staff intends to erect an interpretive display, but if they have not yet, you'll have to search around for the oil well. When the well was rediscovered after the turn of the century, the rotting wooden casing was replaced with a pipe and a screw cap.

Oil and, in later years, gas became big business in the Big South Fork region. But the two largest extraction industries were timbering and coal mining. Cutting trees for lumber occurred on a small scale probably as far back as when the first communities took shape, and coal mining occurred at least as early at 1838.

Once these two industries began to expand, they contributed to a steady increase in the region's population. The last group of immigrants were the managers and workers needed to run the railroads, coal mines, and lumbering operations of a large industrial development that occurred

The People of the Big South Fork

Coal mining in the Big South Fork area (Courtesy of Stearns Museum)

between 1900 and 1930. The development was made possible by the completion in 1880 of the Southern Railway, which linked Cincinnati with Chattanooga. People and equipment could arrive by rail, and coal and lumber could be shipped out.

The largest operation was the Stearns Coal and Lumber Company founded in 1902 by Justus S. Stearns, a Michigan industrialist. The coal and lumber companies were at first separate but later merged. Stearns, Kentucky, was founded as the headquarters of the company, which eventually commanded many thousands of acres of land in the Big South Fork region. The company's band sawmill for cutting lumber was located at Stearns.

In its peak year of 1929, the Stearns Company produced 1,000,000 tons of coal and 18,000,000 board feet of lumber. It employed maybe 2000 miners and several hundred loggers, including many of the local people. To get this lumber and coal from the backwoods to the Southern Railroad line at Stearns, the company had established its own Kentucky and Tennessee Railroad, which ran down into the Big South Fork gorge and then followed the river north to cross on a ballast-filled, concrete arch bridge at Yamacraw erected in 1907; the train then proceeded up Rock Creek.

Top: Lumber stacked to dry at Stearns Lumber Mill (Courtesy of
Stearns Museum)
Bottom: Stearns band sawmill (Courtesy of Stearns Museum)

The People of the Big South Fork

K&T train on bridge at Yamacraw (Courtesy of Stearns Museum)

A number of company towns were established along the K&T to support the industry—Worley, Barthell, and Yamacraw among them. Since there was not much level land in the valleys, and the rail line and the mining operations took up most of that, the towns stretched along the stream banks and up the mountainside on stilts.

The Stearns Company was relatively benevolent, establishing schools in the work camps, not requiring workers to live in company housing, and encouraging the workers to continue farming by being willing to hire part-time, leasing land to those who had none, and establishing a demonstration farm just outside of town. Health care in the camps was often better than in the surrounding rural areas.

While the Stearns Company strongly resisted unionization of their miners, the wages it paid were comparable to what the unions were asking and the mines were some of the safest in the country. In addition, Stearns often led the way in mining technology; by 1914 the company mined with electric equipment. As a result, many miners were already

Worley Coal Camp (Courtesy of Stearns Museum)

The People of the Big South Fork

satisfied working for the Stearns company, but the unions tried to organize anyway. The company's resistance to unionization included intentionally burning the company's hotel in Stearns to route union leaders who were occupying the building and who had killed the federal marshall trying to enforce a warrant. Because of the resistance of the company and their fellow miners, those who wanted to hold union meetings often gathered in the refuge of rock shelters, following in the tradition of the Indian hunting parties, the long hunters, and the early settlers of the region.

In the Tennessee region, the Tennessee Stave and Lumber Company and the New River Lumber Company were the largest operations. The Oneida & Western Railroad served to link Tennessee Stave's logging operations with the Southern Railway line in Oneida; the rail line crossed the Big South Fork on a 200-foot Whipple Truss bridge that was salvaged from another location and erected over the river in 1914 or 1915. Independent lumbering and mining operations also

O&W Railroad (Courtesy of Audney Lloyd)

Top: Train at O&W Depot in Oneida (Courtesy of Audney Lloyd)
Bottom: O&W Depot in Oneida (Courtesy of Audney Lloyd)

Top: O&W Engine #20 (Courtesy of Audney Lloyd)
Bottom: O&W Engine #26 sitting at shop in Oneida (Courtesy of Audney Lloyd)

Exploring the Big South Fork

O&W Bridge from O&W Overlook

opened along the new railroad, which eventually ran as far west as Jamestown. Small communities and camps like Toomey, Gernt, and Zenith grew up around the stops along the O&W where coal and lumber were loaded into the rail cars. The Tennessee Stave bandmill stood on the rail line just west of Oneida at Verdun, named for Verdun, France, which withstood repeated German assaults in World War I. The New River Company had a mill at the community of New River and a larger mill farther east at Norma.

For a time, the region experienced an economic boom. But with the Depression of the 1930s that resulted in a lack of demand for coal and lumber, the economic prospects declined. The downturn also resulted from the easily accessible timber and coal becoming exhausted and from conflicts between labor and management. The demands of World War II provided some reprieve, but the industries were never to fully recover. By 1948, the outmigration had begun. Stearns closed its Yamacraw mines in 1949 and the Worley mines in 1953.

Stearns had opened its Blue Heron Mining operation in 1938 to bolster its operations. A number of mines were located along both sides of the river. Smaller in population than many of the older mining camps because of the use of state-of-the-art technology, Blue Heron operated until 1962, producing over 5 million tons of coal. The output was enough to keep mines operating but never reached expected levels. Stearns sold its last mining operations, which were outside the Big South Fork boundaries, in 1975.

The coal company towns, the lumber mills, and rail lines gradually disappeared. Some coal mining continued, along with oil and gas exploration. But for the most part, the forest and river gorge were left in silence to heal.

TRACES AND SITES OF EXTRACTIVE INDUSTRIES

Exploring some of the back roads in the BSFNRRA, you can occasionally still see an oil pumping station with tanks, or pipes and a manifold emerging from a natural gas line. Both oil and gas production are still allowed within the park boundaries in the adjacent rim area, but not in the gorge area; operations are presently located mostly in the southern area of the park. There are currently 294 oil and gas well sites within the national area. The Park Service monitors this use of the park to ensure sites and roads are properly constructed and reclaimed.

Second-growth timber now hides the effects of the lumbering operations that cut most of the forests of the Big South Fork. Driving some of the back roads in the southern part of the park or along the highways outside the park, you'll occasionally see pine monocultures that remain from more recent lumbering operations.

In contrast, you can still see many of the remains of the mining industry. You can visit the old Blue Heron Mining Community in the Kentucky portion of the park by either driving KY742 and Mine 18 Road down to the community or riding the Big South Fork Scenic Railway that follows the old K&T line from Stearns down to Blue Heron. Before reaching the mining community, the train crosses over Roaring Paunch Creek on a trestle that was originally on the New York Central Railway at Lyon, New York; girders and steel support towers were salvaged and the bridge was erected here in 1937. If you're driving down to Blue Heron, you'll see the trestle to the right where the train tracks cross the road and you make a sharp left curve to enter the community.

You'll find at Blue Heron a reconstructed historic site. Originally all that remained was the tipple, a giant contraption for screening coal into different sizes that began operation in 1938; the vibrating screens and conveyors were driven by nineteen motors. The separated and picked over coal dropped down chutes into railroad cars below to be hauled out of the river gorge. The rest of the community had disappeared through dismantling and decay, but 12 of the old buildings and houses have been resurrected as "ghost" structures, roofs on pilings to give you an idea of what the community once looked like. You can walk the short Blue Heron Trail that takes you through the community. You'll find especially intriguing the recorded voices of the people who lived and worked in the community; within each of the structures you push a button to play the recordings; each has a different theme having to do with the way of life there.

Behind the old tipple, you'll find one of the entrances to Mine 18, also called the "Blue Heron Mine." "Blue Heron" was the Stearns Company

K&T Engine #11 at Blue Heron (Courtesy of Stearns Museum)

K&T train on trestle over Roaring Paunch Creek (Courtesy of Stearns Museum)

Top: Blue Heron Tipple (Courtesy of Stearns Museum)
Bottom: Tram bridge at Blue Heron (Courtesy of Stearns Museum)

Gated mine near Blue Heron

name for an intermediate grade of coal. You can also walk across the top of the tipple and then across the tram bridge that crosses the river, a total span of 975 feet. The coal company once hauled coal from mines along both sides of the river by tramcars pulled by electric motors. The bridge allowed the tramcars from the west side to cross the river and pass over the tipple where the drop-bottom cars released their loads.

The bridge now gives access to hiking trails that follow the old tram railbeds on the west side of the river. Following the hiking trail north along the old tramroad for about 0.3 mile, you'll begin to see upright posts that remain from the line of utility poles that carried electricity along the tram track. South along the tramroad you'll see discarded tramcars beside the trail on the left and coal littered along the path.

A section of trail turns left off this main trail south at 0.2 mile that has been abandoned because of slides. A proposal calls for fixing the trail. When it reopens as part of the Catawba Overlook Loop, you'll be able to continue following the old tramline bed past a gated mine opening.

Hiking any of the trails in the area, you'll likely see streams stained bright orange or yellow-brown. This is the result of acid mine drainage; when acid water flowing from a coal mine makes contact with the air, iron sulfate precipitates out. This precipitate, called "yellow boy," gives the stream its discoloration. The Park Service has an active project to address the yellow-boy problem.

Most mined areas in the park have been reclaimed. From the Devil's Jump Overlook, you'll see a reclaimed spoils pile below. A field of debris was dumped there from a mine, but the area has been reclaimed with topsoil and perennial grasses and, at the upper end, a stand of pine trees.

Big South Fork Structures Eligible for the National Register of Historic Places

Historic American Building Survey

Charit Creek Lodge on Station Camp Creek
John Blevins Four-Crib Barn at Charit Creek Lodge
John Blevins Corncrib at Charit Creek Lodge
John Blevins Log Blacksmith Shop at Charit Creek Lodge
John B. Blevins Log House at Oscar Blevins Farm Site
John B. Blevins Corncrib at Oscar Blevins Farm Site
Lora E. Blevins Log House at Clara Sue Blevins Site
Lora E. Blevins Log Barn at Clara Sue Blevins Site
Lora E. Blevins Corncrib at Clara Sue Blevins Site
John Litton Log House at John Litton (General Slaven) Farm
John Litton English-Style Barn at John Litton (General Slaven) Farm
John Litton Cabin on Parch Corn Creek

Historic American Engineering Resources

K&T Bridge over the Big South Fork at Yamacraw
K&T Trestle over Roaring Paunch Creek near Blue Heron
Blue Heron Tipple at the Blue Heron Mining Community
O&W Bridge over the Big South Fork south of Leatherwood Ford
Low-water bridge at Leatherwood Ford

From Devil's Jump Overlook

South Arch

Virginia Bluebell

SONDRA JAMIESON

Angel Falls

White-tailed Deer

AL FOSTER

Trout Lily

SONDRA JAMIESON

O&W Overlook

SONDRA JAMIESON

Horseback Riding

Flame Azalea

River at Bear Creek

Fall Color

Charit Creek Lodge

Needle Arch

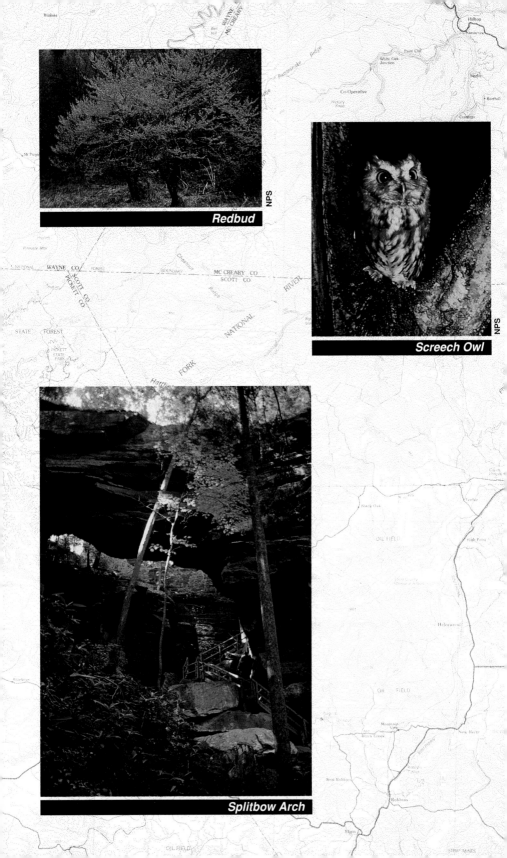

Redbud

NPS

Screech Owl

NPS

Splitbow Arch

Bloodroot

Kayaking Double Falls

Blue Heron Tipple

Yahoo Falls

Gray Fox Pups

NPS

O&W Bridge

SONDRA JAMIESON

Fall Color

John B. Blevins Log House

SONDRA JAMIESON

Rock Shelter

Mountain Laurel

East Tunnel

Fishing at Leatherwood Ford

Trail's End

White-footed Mouse

NPS

Fall Branch

Mountain Biking

Outdoor
Activities

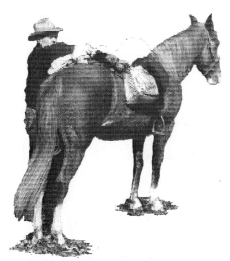

The Big South Fork National River and Recreation Area is one of the best places for outdoor recreation in the eastern United States. The outdoor activities are as numerous as you have imagination to invent. Here are the more popular ones.

HIKING

Perhaps hiking is the most popular activity in the park and the easiest in which to participate. Even if you come to the park for some other outdoor activity, you'll probably end up taking a stroll through the woods to see a natural arch or an overlook or just to stretch your legs.

There are about 200 miles of designated hiking trails in the BSFNRRA. The trails range from less than a mile to as much as 40 miles in length; most are suitable for day hikes. Many can be combined for long hikes and backpacking trips. Hikers may also use the horse trails, but you should give horses the right of way by quietly standing to the lower side of the trail and allowing them to pass. In addition, old roads in the park are interesting to explore.

Before setting out on a hike, make sure you have a map of the trail you are taking and the surrounding area. Also, you'll need the basic shoes, clothing, rain gear, water, lunch, insect repellent, and first aid kit

Hiking John Muir Trail from O&W Bridge

described earlier in the section on what to bring when visiting the park. Just in case you get lost, you should also take along a compass, extra clothes, a knife, a flashlight, and a lighter or waterproof matches plus some fire starter for building a fire. If you do get lost or need to make an injured person comfortable, you'll also be glad if you brought along a plastic sheet or emergency blanket.

Trail maps are available through the Visitor Center, where you can also purchase one of the hiking guides for detailed directions. You might secure a map and hiking guide prior to coming to the park so you can plan ahead. Read through the trail descriptions, plan your route, and study the trail connections while looking at an overall map of the park. The park rangers will be glad to give you additional information about a trail and the current conditions.

All the designated hiking trails in the Big South Fork are marked with a red arrowhead in a white blaze, with the exceptions of the John Muir Trail, which has a blue silhouette of Muir on a white blaze; the Sheltowee Trace, which has a white or sometimes blue turtle and white diamonds; the Yahoo Falls trails, which have yellow, green, and blue blazes; and occasionally a connector trail that has an arrowhead blaze of blue or gray. The blazes are usually spaced close enough that you will see one ahead whenever you begin to wonder if you have strayed from the trail. You might also look behind to see a blaze headed in the other direction to assure yourself that you are still on the trail.

If you ask or read about the difficulty of a trail, you'll usually be told that it is easy, moderate, or difficult. The degree of difficulty is usually based on the ability of an average person, someone who occasionally hikes but for whom a long hike is not a frequent occurrence. So more experienced hikers may find what are described as moderate hikes quite easy and the difficult hikes fairly moderate. Someone who rarely hikes will find the moderate and perhaps the easy trails difficult.

A rating is usually based on a subjective judgment of the strenuousness of the trail—how much up and down there is, how difficult are the stream crossings, whether the footing on the trail is rocky or overgrown. As a result, while a 10-mile trail would be difficult for anyone not used to hiking, it might be called easy if it is relatively level, has no creek crossings, and is fairly easy walking. So if you are not accustomed to hiking, look not only at the degree of difficulty, but also at the distance you will walk (double that if the trail does not form a loop; you'll also have to walk back). You might also ask about any particular areas of caution that you will encounter on a trail, such as creek crossings, rocky footing, mudholes, steep climbs and descents. When deciding whether you're up to hiking a particular trail, you'll need to take these cautions into consideration and be prepared.

Once at the trailhead, you should be able to find your way by following a map and reading the signs at most trail junctions. But you are expected to assume responsibility for knowing where you are going and for not getting lost. Always let someone know where you are going and give them an expected return time so he or she can contact park authorities if you don't show up. To keep from getting lost, watch for trail signs and blazes, stay on the trails, and don't over estimate your ability. Hiking in plateau canyon country can be difficult because of the rugged terrain; inexperienced hikers often under estimate the difficulty and so also under estimate the time required to cover a trail. If while hiking you do not know where to go forward, but remember the way you came, you might try backtracking until you reach a location in which you know where you are, rather than continuing forward and becoming more confused. Do not leave the trail if you get lost; search teams will cover the trails first when looking for you.

To help preserve the area, do not cut across switchbacks; taking shortcuts that others then follow causes erosion. And resist the temptation to skirt muddy areas; walking around widens the trail and destroys vegetation.

It is best to hike with someone. Then if one of you falls or turns an ankle, someone will be there to care for the injured person. If the injured cannot make it back to the trailhead, make the person warm and comfortable, leave someone to tend the person if there is a third hiker in your party, pay attention to the exact location, and then hike out and contact the park rangers who will help in rescuing the injured.

Stream crossings can be quite easy or quite difficult. Many crossings have sturdy bridges, but many others do not and you may have to ford.

After a heavy rain, a stream can be swollen with rushing water and is often more hazardous than it appears. Do not attempt to cross such a stream unless you are sure you can make it. When the water level is down, you'll find that you can rockhop most streams, but this can also be hazardous if the rocks are wet; use caution and be prepared to slip. If you decide to wade across, wear your shoes to protect your feet; some hikers carry along old tennis shoes to slip into for stream crossings. Find a stick to use for balance. If you're carrying a pack, release the waist strap so you can slip out of the pack easily in case you fall. If you do take a dunking and the water carries you away, orient yourself to float on your back with your feet downstream so you can ward off rocks until you have a chance to stop yourself and get out of the water. Even when you are crossing a footbridge over a creek you should use caution; some can be wet and slippery or in winter covered with ice.

Be prepared for a change in the weather. On cooler days dress in layers so you can adjust your clothes as you warm up or cool down. And it rains frequently on the Plateau; so you should always have rain gear.

Review all the precautions on snakes, insects, poison ivy, hypothermia, and emergencies mentioned earlier in the section on Planning a Visit. Don't be discouraged from walking the trails by all these warnings. The Big South Fork is well worth having to take a few precautions.

In addition to the trails listed in the accompanying chart, many miles of proposed hiking trails will be constructed in the future. Watch for new trails out of the Bear Creek Scenic Area, the Ledbetter Trailhead, and a new Slavens Branch Trailhead in Kentucky and, in Tennessee, new trails out of Burnt Mill, Zenith, Station Camp East, and a new trailhead on Terry Cemetery Road off Divide Road in the Middle Creek area.

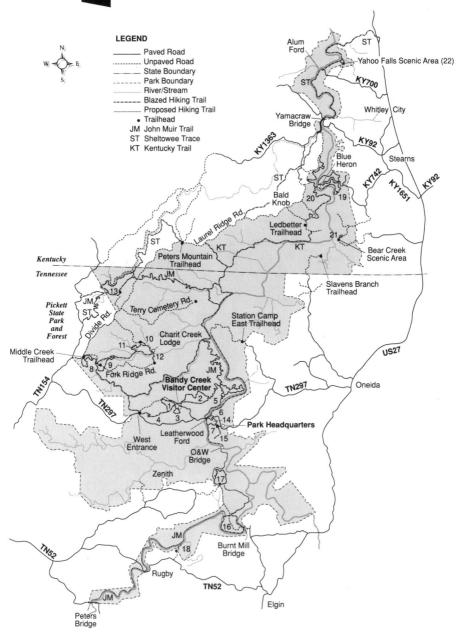

LEGEND
_____ Paved Road
·············· Unpaved Road
_____ State Boundary
------ Park Boundary
·············· River/Stream
·············· Blazed Hiking Trail
·············· Proposed Hiking Trail
• Trailhead
JM John Muir Trail
ST Sheltowee Trace
KT Kentucky Trail

Alum Ford
ST
Yahoo Falls Scenic Area (22)
KY700
ST
Whitley City
Yamacraw Bridge
KY1363
KY92
Blue Heron
Stearns
ST
KY742
KY1651
KY92
Bald Knob
20
19
Ledbetter Trailhead
21
Bear Creek Scenic Area
Laurel Ridge Rd.
ST
KT
KT
Kentucky
Peters Mountain Trailhead
Slavens Branch Trailhead
Tennessee
JM
JM
13
Pickett State Park and Forest
ST
Terry Cemetery Rd.
Divide Rd.
Station Camp East Trailhead
Middle Creek Trailhead
10
Charit Creek Lodge
11
12
US27
9
8
Fork Ridge Rd.
JM
TN154
Bandy Creek Visitor Center
TN297
Oneida
TN297
2
5
1
6
4
3
14
Park Headquarters
West Entrance
Leatherwood Ford
7
15
O&W Bridge
Zenith
17
16
JM
18
Burnt Mill Bridge
TN52
Rugby
TN52
JM
Elgin
Peters Bridge

Hiking Trails of the Big South Fork

Exploring the Big South Fork

Favorite Hiking Trails at the Big South Fork

1   The easy 3.6-mile **Oscar Blevins Farm Loop** leads from the Bandy Creek Trailhead to circle by the Blevins Farm; the trailhead is just down the road from the Visitor Center, on the left.

2   The moderate 5.9-mile **John Litton Farm Loop** passes through the Litton homeplace; also from the Bandy Creek Trailhead or from the parking area next to the swimming pool.

3   The easy 1.3-mile **Bandy Creek Loop Trail** is a graveled path that begins at the Bandy Creek Visitor Center and circles the stables and fields through an Uplands Forest.

4   The easy 2.4-mile **West Entrance-Bandy Creek Trail** one-way connects the West Entrance Trailhead just inside the West Entrance on TN297 to the Oscar Blevins Farm Loop.

5   A moderate 3.0-mile section of the John Muir Trail one-way north from Leatherwood Ford on TN297 reaches the splendid **Angel Falls Overlook** of the Big South Fork.

6   The easy 2.0-mile **Angel Falls Trail** one-way north from Leatherwood Ford leads to a view of the rapids. Continuing north on this trail you'll reach Station Camp Ford in another 6.1 miles; the entire trail along the east side of the river will be called "River Trail East."

7   The moderate 2.3-mile section of the John Muir Trail one way south from Leatherwood Ford arrives at the **O&W Railroad Bridge** over the Big South Fork.

8   The moderate 3.5-mile **Middle Creek Nature Trail** from the Middle Creek Trailhead on Divide Road on the west side of the park passes by numerous rock shelters as it forms a loop.

9   The easy 4.2-mile **Slave Falls Loop** from the Sawmill Trailhead on Fork Ridge Road in the Middle Creek area swings by Slave Falls and Indian Rock House.

10   The easy 0.7-mile one-way **Twin Arches Trail** from the Twin Arches Trailhead on Divide Road leads to these massive arches.

Outdoor Activities

11 The moderate 4.6-mile **Twin Arches/Charit Creek Loop** off the Twin Arches Trail circles by Jake's Place and Charit Creek Lodge.

12 The moderate 0.8-mile one-way **Charit Creek Lodge Trail** leads from the end of Fork Ridge Road down to Charit Creek Lodge.

13 The moderate 8-mile **Rock Creek Loop** that descends along an old railroad bed to Rock Creek begins at the Hattie Blevins Cemetery in the Middle Creek area; take Divide Road north to Three Forks and turn left to reach the cemetery and trailhead.

14 The moderate 3.2-mile **Leatherwood Ford Loop** from the East Rim Trailhead on the East Rim Overlook Road off TN297 leads to an overlook of Leatherwood Ford and descends to the river before looping back to the top of the plateau.

15 The easy 1.3-mile one-way **Sunset Overlook Trail**, also from the East Rim Trailhead, leads to another overlook of the river.

16 The moderate 4.3-mile **Burnt Mill Bridge Loop** from the Burnt Mill Bridge River Access follows along the Clear Fork River.

17 The difficult 5.2-mile **Honey Creek Loop** from the Honey Creek Trailhead provides one of the most interesting and intricate hikes in the park.

18 The moderate 1-mile one-way **Gentlemen's Swimming Hole Trail** at Rugby takes you down to the old swimming hole on the Clear Fork River; from TN52 in the historic community, turn north on the road to Laurel Dale Cemetery where you'll find the trailhead across from the cemetery.

19 The moderate 6.6-mile **Blue Heron Loop** out of the Blue Heron Mining Community passes through Cracks-in-the-Rock and circles around to the Devil's Jump Rapids.

20 The moderate 1.6-mile one-way hike to **Catawba Overlook** follows the old tramroad on the west side of the river at Blue Heron; this route is part of the Kentucky Trail; at the Blue Heron Mining Community, walk across the tram bridge to the other side of the river and turn south to reach the overlook of the river gorge; you can continue south another 2.1 miles to pass Dick Gap Falls and reach Big Spring Falls.

21 The easy 0.7-mile **Split Bow Arch Loop** in the Bear Creek Scenic Area passes through Split Bow Arch.

22 The moderate 0.8-mile **Topside Loop** and the moderate 0.2-mile **Cascade Loop** in the Yahoo Falls Scenic Area circle by Yahoo Falls and Roaring Rocks Cataract; there's also an easy 1.2-mile one-way **Yahoo Arch Trail** that leads into the surrounding national forest land to a large natural arch.

BACKPACKING

If you want to hike long distances or just spend more time experiencing the Big South Fork, you'll probably want to backpack. Being out for several days at a time provides a rich experience and a good escape from the harried life.

The best backpacking trail in the park is the John Muir Trail, named for the noted conservationist who in 1867 explored this Cumberland region before heading west to crusade for the establishment of national parks and found the Sierra Club. The easiest southern access for the Muir Trail is at Leatherwood Ford. The trail then travels north for 40 miles passing through some of the most isolated backcountry in the park to end at Pickett State Rustic Park just outside the BSFNRRA on the west. From Leatherwood Ford, the John Muir Trail also heads south on the east side of the river 2.3 miles to the O&W Bridge where it currently ends; but work has started on an extension of the trail south to the Burnt Mill Bridge area of the park where a small section of the trail now exists and should be completed in 1994. Connection with this southern portion will add another 7 miles or so. Plans for the John Muir Trail call for it to eventually be extended south all the way to the Peters Bridge River Access at the southern boundary of the park. That will add another 16 miles to the total length of the trail.

You'll find more remote backpacking along the 27-mile Kentucky

Trail that begins at the Peters Mountain Trailhead. On the west side of the park, take Divide Road off TN154 east into the Middle Creek area. Stay with Divide Road, which becomes Peters Mountain Road when it crosses the state line, for 11 miles to the trailhead. The trail begins northeast on the Laurel Ridge Road but soon turns southeast off the road to cross the northern area of the park and pass through the Ledbetter Place Trailhead on Bald Knob Road. The trail continues north, past the tram bridge across the river to the Blue Heron Mining Community and on to emerge on Wilson Ridge Road and then follow the road north and eventually turn off to connect with the Sheltowee Trace. You can then follow the trace north to Yamacraw Bridge.

The Sheltowee Trace National Recreation Trail also provides for long-distance hiking. The trail is named for Daniel Boone, who was given the name "Sheltowee," meaning "Big Turtle," by the Shawnee, who were holding him captive at the time. This 257-mile trail passes north to south through Kentucky's Daniel Boone National Forest, entering the BSFNRRA at Big Creek on the northern end of the park. The easiest access for this trail section is at the Yahoo Falls Scenic Area. The trail then heads south along the Big South Fork through Alum Ford to cross to the west side at Yamacraw Bridge; a proposal calls for rerouting the trail south from the highway bridge and having it cross the river on the old K&T Railroad Bridge; watch for this change sometime in the future. The trace reenters the Daniel Boone National Forest at Yamacraw and then parallels the northern boundary of the BSFNRRA southwest to eventually follow along Rock Creek and cut through the northwest corner of the park and end at Pickett State Rustic Park at the same point as the John Muir Trail. From the Yahoo Falls Scenic Area to Pickett State Park is a distance of about 42 miles.

For backpacking, you will of course need everything for surviving in the open overnight and for however many days you choose to be out. If you are inexperienced in backpacking, the park rangers or your local outfitters can give advice on the equipment needed. Your first time out, you should go with someone experienced in backpacking. Keep in mind all the precautions mentioned in the section on hiking.

At the minimum, you should have along a trail map that gives you an overall view of the park and the trail connections. But you'll probably want more detailed information than a trail map provides. So also look at the topographical maps that cover the area you will be hiking. The most useful are the 1:24,000 quads (the 7.5 minute series). Topographical maps are available from your local map supplier or at the park Visitor Center.

Plan ahead. Read through the trail descriptions in a hiking guide prior to going, plan your route, and study the trail connections while looking at an overall map of the park. Ask the rangers about the current conditions of the trails and about any problem areas, such as stream crossings that do not have bridges. Use the normal precautions when crossing streams; be sure to release the hip belt of your backpack when fording so you can easily slip out of the pack if you fall in the water.

Backcountry registration is not required at this time, but you'll be

Backpacking at the Big South Fork (Courtesy of the NPS)

Outdoor Activities

wise to let a ranger know your plans. You can register at the Bandy Creek Visitor Center and the Blue Heron Mining Community or by calling 615/879-3625. At least let a friend or member of your family know where you intend to be so they can contact the park staff if you get into trouble and do not return when expected.

It is best to backpack with someone. Then if one of you is injured, a person will be there to care for the injured person and to go for help.

You may camp virtually anywhere in the backcountry, but set up at least 25 feet from trails, gravel and dirt roads, rock shelters, the gorge rim, and major geologic and historic features and at least 100 feet from streams and the center line of paved roads, 200 feet from parking lots and other developed areas and only if you cannot be seen, and 200 feet from cemeteries and gravesites. If you are in a high use area, camp at an existing site rather than damage vegetation at a new site. In more remote areas, pick the site where you will cause the least damage. Near streams, and especially near the river, set up camp on a high area to avoid rising flood waters from rain upstream. Some areas that receive overuse may be closed, such as currently at Jake's Place on the Twin Arches/Charit Creek Loop. At the established campgrounds, camping is permitted only in designated sites.

You should plan to camp in the vicinity of a large stream to be guaranteed of a source of water; streams are noted on the maps. You can of course also get water from streams while you are hiking during the day. You'll need to also carry water with you in case you do not find a flowing stream. Purify all water in the backcountry.

When camping, use only down and dead timber for campfires; build your fires on cleared ground and be sure to douse your fire with water and then make sure the coals are cold before leaving. Scatter the ashes to hide the site unless it is a designated camping area or has a frequently used fire ring. You may gather nuts and berries in reasonable quantities for your personal use, but make sure you know what you're eating; some berries and nuts are toxic.

At night, hang your food on a rope between two trees to keep it away from animals. Bury your waste at least six inches deep and 100 feet away from trails, water sources, and campsites. Do not bury sanitary napkins or tampons; instead, add them to your trash bag and carry them out. Do not wash dishes in a stream; take water from the streams to do your washing and let the waste water drain onto the ground. Use the same procedure if you plan on bathing with soap instead of just splashing around in the water.

When breaking camp, take down any ropes or branches you have used in making camp. Pack out all trash and litter. And take a last look to ensure you have left no trace of having been there.

CROSSCOUNTRY HIKING

Hiking crosscountry has its special rewards. This is true exploring, perhaps going where no one has set foot before, except maybe the Native Americans who once hunted the region. You may discover a unknown arch and or an unseen waterfall.

You should not attempt to crosscountry, even if this means just following unmarked old roads, unless you are an experienced hiker and navigator. If you intend to hike where there are no designated trails, you must have a compass and topographical maps and know how to use them together in a process called "orienteering" to determine your location. You will need to be especially careful while walking in areas of steep dropoffs, and of course, do not hike after dark when you can't really see where you're going. You should take with you all the equipment required for backpacking in case you get lost or if you intend to spend the night outside.

Plan ahead and let a ranger know your intended route.

HORSEBACK RIDING

The BSFNRRA is one of the best places in the Southeast for horseback riding. The park has 130 miles of trails specifically designed for horses, and 75-80 miles of new trails are being added at this writing. The horse trails have a yellow or orange silhouette of a horse's head on

Horseback riding at the Big South Fork

a white blaze. Horses may not use the designated hiking or biking trails nor paved roads. And you may not ride crosscountry. But there are something like 180 miles of unmarked roads that you may explore; if a road is grown up in trees and brush or if it is blazed for hiking or mountain biking, it is not considered an existing road and so is not open to horse traffic.

You can get a trail map at the Visitor Center that shows both hiking and horse trails. You should also take along the topographic maps that cover the area of your ride, also available at the Visitor Center; many of the horse trails appear on the topos as old roads.

When you arrive at the park, you must have in your possession proof of a negative Coggins test for swamp fever (EIA) for your horse.

You may want to make the Bandy Creek area your base of operations since many horse trails lead out from this area. At the Bandy Creek Stables (615/879-4013), a concessionaire within the park, you can rent a stall for your horse while you stay in the campground. Charit Creek Lodge also has stables for keeping horses overnight.

You may also rent horses at the Bandy Creek Stables for guided horseback rides of an hour or more or overnight trips of two or three days from April to mid-November, or for long trips in winter by prior arrangement; minimum age is six and maximum weight is 250 lbs. Overnights are spent at a backcountry camp or at Charit Creek Lodge; bring your own sleeping bag and personal items. You must make reservations. Don't forget to wear long pants. The stables also offers wagon rides; contact the stables for details.

In addition to the Bandy Creek complex, new equestrian camps can serve as the base from which to ride. An equestrian camp at Station Camp East will open in 1994; the camping spaces will have water and electricity, hitching posts, and a central bathhouse. Another equestrian camp near the Bear Creek Scenic Area will also open in 1994. An equestrian camp is also scheduled for the Middle Creek area of the park on Fork Ridge Road. These will be fee campgrounds as are the two other established campgrounds in the park. As these new camps become operational, watch for new trailheads and horse trails and possible relocation of existing trailheads. Proposed trails out of the Bear Creek area will connect with Blue Heron to the north and Station Camp East to the south. A number of old roads already penetrate the area north of Station Camp East.

Designated horse trails in the park usually have good signs that help you find your way. Plan your route ahead of time and study the trail connections with a topographical map. Ask the rangers about the current conditions of the trails and about any problem areas, such as stream crossings, river fords, and rock ledges that may be difficult to negotiate. You should let the rangers know where you are going, especially if you are exploring old roads; at least let a friend or member of your family know where you intend to be so they can contact the park staff if you get into trouble and do not return when expected. It is best to ride with someone. Then if one of you is injured, a person will be there to care for the injured person and to go for help.

Check the trail and topographic maps for creek crossings where

Outdoor Activities

your horse can get water. Ask the rangers about recent weather; if there has been no rain recently, some of the creeks may be dry, and so you can ask for recommendations of trails where water will be available. If there has been recent rain, the creeks will be running and puddles along the trail will provide suitable water. When watering at a creek, choose a rocky area along the stream to minimize bank erosion.

Although horses have the right-of-way on horse trails, be aware that hikers and bicycle riders are also allowed to use the trails. A horse can be quite intimidating to someone on the ground; so be courteous when encountering nonhorse people and allow them time to step aside before riding by, at a walk. Some horse-only trails have been proposed for the future.

Remember that a comfortable horse, correctly shod and properly packed, stands quieter and causes less trail wear. You can also minimize trail wear by keeping the horses in your group in single file and so avoid the creation of multiple trails. To avoid widening the trail, don't let your horse unnecessarily skirt shallow puddles and minor obstacles and do not shortcut across switchbacks. Let the park rangers know of blowdowns you encounter so they can be removed before trails are created going around the obstructions. When taking a rest stop, crosstie your horse off the trail to minimize trail wear. Try not to let your horse browse because of the possible presence of endangered plant species. Hitching rails are often provided at locations where you need to walk to a geologic or historic site.

When taking rest stops or camping in the backcountry, horses should be tied on picket lines away from trees, buildings, and at least 100 feet from water sources. You should acquaint your horse with picket ropes, hitch lines, and hobbles prior to your trip so you and the horse will not have trouble in the backcountry. As a courtesy to fellow campers, horses should not be kept in camp, but should be tied some distance away.

You may camp virtually anywhere in the backcountry away from roads and geologic and historic sites. Registration is not required at this time, but it's a good idea to let the rangers know where you intend to go. When selecting a campsite, look for one that can withstand the impact

Getting ready for the trail

of horses and does not have to be cleared of vegetation. Grazing is by permit only. If horses are left to graze, move the picket line frequently to prevent overgrazing. Grazing in the backcountry is limited anyway, so you'll need to bring feed along. When breaking camp, always remove any hitching ropes or picket lines you've tied to trees, scatter your horse's manure, and pack out all trash.

Each spring, the Big South Fork Competitive Ride takes place, sanctioned by the North American Trail Ride Conference and sponsored by the Knoxville Arabian Horse Club. Riders are judged on handling and conditioning of the horse. Contact NATRC (619/588-7245) for details.

In addition to the horse trails mentioned in the accompanying chart, a number of new horse trails have been proposed. Several of these will be accessed out of a new Slavens Branch Trailhead that is under construction at this writing in the Kentucky portion of the park south of the Bear Creek area. To get to this area, turn west off US27 on Litton Road in Oneida 0.9 mile north of the junction of US27 and TN297. In 0.1

Outdoor Activities

mile bear left on Grave Hill Road, and then at 0.5 mile keep right to stay on Grave Hill Road. At 2.1 miles keep left and you'll arrive at Foster Crossroads in 7.4 miles. (Or if you're coming from the park on TN297, at 3.8 miles east of the right turn of TN297 at the Terry and Terry Store, turn north on Williams Creek Road. Then at 4.5 miles turn right on the Pine Creek Baptist Church road; Williams Creek Road continues on to become a four-wheel drive road that fords Williams Creek and connects with the Station Camp Road. After passing the Pine Creek Baptist Church on the side road, you'll connect with the Grave Hill Road at 5.9 miles. Continue left on Grave Hill another 5 miles to Foster Crossroads.) At the Foster Cross Road Baptist Church, take the far right gravel road 1.0 mile down to cross the state line into Kentucky and also the boundary of the park onto Little Bill Slaven Road. At 2.1 miles you'll pass Hulling Branch Road on the left and reach the end of the Slaven Road at 3.2 miles; the road could become muddy in wet weather if it has not been improved. The new trailhead will be located a little before the end of the road. Check with the park Visitor Center for whether this trailhead is now operational.

Popular Horse Trails at the Big South Fork

1   The 18.5-mile **North White Oak Loop** starts at the Bandy Creek Equestrian Trailhead along the South Bandy Creek Trail south to the loop part of the ride and crosses TN297; a soft and sandy tread, level to gentle hills. The trail takes you by a 1.6-mile side trail to an overlook of North White Oak Creek and a 2.3-mile side trail to an overlook of Leatherwood Ford; the loop plus the trails to the overlooks and back total 26.3 miles. For a shorter route, you can go just to the Leatherwood Overlook and back for a 10.4-mile ride. To get to the Bandy Creek Trailhead, continue on the Bandy Creek Road past the Visitor Center and turn left just before the pavement ends; you'll pass a parking area and restrooms for the hiking trailhead and continue on to the equestrian trailhead; you'll see a corral there available for day use only.

2   You can also take the **Coyle Branch Trail** off the North White Oak Loop south along the old Coyle Branch Road toward North White Oak Creek and

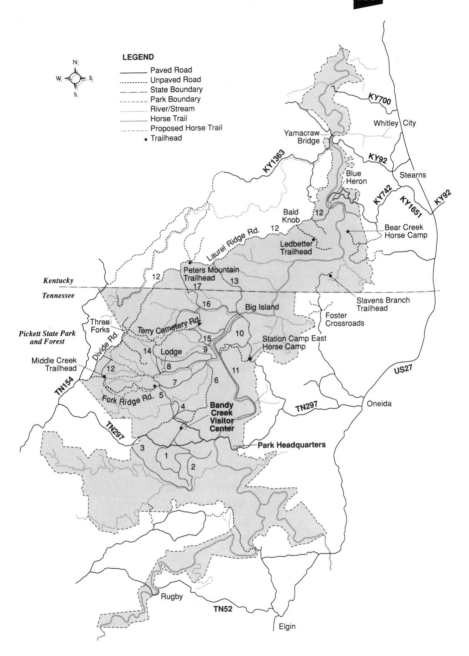

Horse Trails of the Big South Fork

Outdoor Activities

descend to the old O&W Railroad bed in about 5 miles; be aware the descent is rough and rocky. You can make a loop ride by then turning west on the O&W Railbed to the Gernt Trail and returning to the North White Oak Loop for a total of about 14 miles.

3   The 6-mile **Gernt Trail** begins as a small road track on the east side of the Hitching Post Grocery that's 1 mile outside the west park boundary. Following the Gernt Road, the trail enters the park and heads south toward North White Oak Creek, descending to the railbed; a tough descent, rocky and rough. Proposed trails will connect the Gernt Trail with the North White Oak Loop, giving easier access to the Gernt Trail.

4   The 6-mile **Jacks Ridge Loop** begins at the Bandy Creek Equestrian Trailhead or the end of the Jacks Ridge Road that can be reached by continuing on the Bandy Creek Road 1.3 miles from the Visitor Center and turning north on the Jacks Ridge Road for 0.8 mile; a soft and sandy tread, level to gentle hills; the loop makes use of the Jacks Ridge Road.

5   The **Charit Creek Horse Trail** from the Bandy Creek Equestrian Trailhead is 3.6 miles, or from the end of the Jacks Ridge Road is 3.0 miles, to the Charit Creek Lodge where you can spend the night with reservations; good tread and good water; fords Laurel Fork, Black House Branch, and Station Camp Creek (this ride uses the North Bandy Creek Trail to the Clara Sue Blevins Trail west and part of the Jacks Ridge Loop north; the section then connecting Jacks Ridge Loop and Fork Ridge Road will be called the "Black House Branch Trail"). You'll cross Fork Ridge Road 1.5 miles before reaching the lodge so you could start your ride from the Charit Creek Equestrian Trailhead 0.4 mile to the east up Fork Ridge Road for quick access to Charit Creek.

6   The **Duncan Hollow Trail**, accessed from the Bandy Creek Equestrian Trailhead by the North Bandy Creek and the Clara Sue Blevins Trails, leads 6 miles along the old Duncan Hollow Road to Station Camp Creek; smooth tread often muddy in wet weather; fords Laurel Fork and Station Camp Creek near the end to connect with the Station Camp Creek Trail. Beginning at the Bandy Creek Campground, the Duncan Hollow Road is open to vehicles for the first 4.2 miles.

7   The **Fork Ridge Trail** follows the old Fork Ridge Road east from its intersection with the Charit Creek Horse Trail 3.5 miles to a junction with the

Duncan Hollow Trail; good tread until the roadbed becomes a steep, rocky trail with ledges leading down toward Laurel Fork; you should get off and lead your horse through this difficult section (it has been proposed that this section be eliminated by rerouting the trail north to ford Station Camp Creek and connect with the Station Camp Creek Trail where you can continue eastward). The Charit Creek Horse Trail and the Fork Ridge and Duncan Hollow Trails make an 11.6-mile loop.

8   The **Station Camp Creek Trail** leads from Charit Creek Lodge 3.1 miles east to a junction with the Duncan Hollow Trail and, 0.8 mile beyond, to the Station Camp river ford; smooth and sandy tread with little elevation but several crossings of Station Camp Creek. At the river you can ford to connect with the Big Island Loop; make the river crossing to the east side only at low water (you'll need to skirt a section of big rocks instead of making the crossing straight across). The Station Camp Creek Trail, Duncan Hollow Trail, and Charit Creek Horse Trail can be combined for a 12.7-mile loop ride.

9   The 9.7-mile **Hatfield Ridge Loop** from Charit Creek Lodge follows the Station Camp Creek Trail east but then, before reaching the river, turns north up Hatfield Ridge to circle back to the lodge with views and a side trail to the Charit Creek Overlook along the way; good tread; steep grades ascending and descending the ridge.

10   The 11-mile **Big Island Loop** (or Station Camp East Loop) begins at the Station Camp river ford or can be reached by a 1.6-mile connecting trail from the Station Camp East Trailhead on the Station Camp Road (also watch for a connector trail from the new equestrian camp); smooth and sandy on the plateau, variable along the river with some mud and rock, steep descent to Big Island with rocks and ledges but negotiable, and steep ascent from Station Camp Ford with good tread. You'll pass a side trail to interesting Dome Rockhouse with a hitching rail in shade. At Big Island you can ford the river to connect with the Long Trail, but it's muddy on both sides of the river; ford only at low water. On the east side of the river about a mile south of Big Island stands the Burke Cabin, a hunting and fishing cabin built in the 1970s that has been rehabilitated by volunteers and may be used for overnight stays.

11   From the Station Camp river ford, you can also head south along the **River Trail East** for 6.0 miles for access to Angel Falls; you must hitch your horse and walk the last bit to get to the view of the rapids. This trail has traditionally been a hiking trail, but because of little use by the hikers, it has been opened for horse travel to provide access to this scenic spot.

12   The **Long Trail** combines several trails for a long ride. From the Middle Creek Equestrian Trailhead (or Long Trailhead), which is on Fork Ridge Road 1.8 miles from TN154, ride north on the Three Forks Trail to reach the Middle Creek Trail, which follows the old Middle Creek Road (southeast, the old road leads toward Charit Creek Lodge); turn northwest on the Middle Creek Trail to connect with Divide Road (hard packed and gravel) that leads northeast through Three Forks (the Three Forks Trail will eventually run all the way to Three Forks). Stay northeast on Divide Road to the Kentucky/Tennessee State Line where it becomes the Peters Mountain Road and continue on to the Peters Mountain Trailhead, where you can also begin rides. The trail then continues along the Laurel Ridge Road through a couple of turns (hard packed but muddy after rain, rock ledges) to Bald Knob, past the Bald Knob Road, and then beyond to turn down the Waters Cemetery Road. Soon after, you'll turn north to head to Blue Heron in a total of 22.9 miles (you must descend a steep rocky roadbed and ford the river to get across to Blue Heron at the river access ramp; a hiking trail leading to the tram bridge over the river has been proposed as multiple use so you may at some future time be able to take your horses to the beginning of the bridge and hitch them there while you walk across the bridge to visit the mining community). The last part of the Long Trail may at some time be rerouted to turn down Bald Knob Road to the Ledbetter Trailhead and then turn north along a new Dick Gap Trail to Blue Heron. A number of new trails are also proposed for off Laurel Ridge Road and out of the Ledbetter Trailhead. Once you ford across to Blue Heron, you can turn east on the Blue Heron Trail that leads to Laurel Branch where new trails will eventually connect with the Bear Creek area; now an old road leads up to the Mine 18 Road.

13   The **Big Island Branch Loop of the Long Trail** turns off the Laurel Ridge Road at Stepping Rock along a trail that will be designated the Difficulty Creek Trail. The ride then turns southeast toward Big Island along the Miller Branch Trail (variable tread with ledges and a 3-foot dropoff that should be walked) and then south along the river, passing the John Litton Cabin on Parch Corn Creek, and on to Station Camp Creek where you'll then use the Station Camp Creek Trail to head west to Charit Creek Lodge; the section of trail south from Big Island is being eroded by the river and so you should watch for a rerouting in the future.

From the lodge, you can then head up the Charit Creek Horse Trail to Fork Ridge Road and follow it west to return to the Middle Creek Equestrian Trailhead to form a 28-mile loop; a proposed westward extension of the Fork Ridge Trail will parallel the road. On Fork Ridge Road, you'll pass the Charit Creek Equestrian Trailhead where you can also begin the ride. A future alternative route from the lodge will be to turn on the old Middle Creek Road off the Charit Creek Horse Trail and then turn on the Booger Blevins Trail that follows an old road back to the trailhead.

14 A shorter **Hatfield Ridge Branch Loop of the Long Trail** forms a 12.4-mile circuit by turning south off Divide Road at Three Forks on the Terry Cemetery Road. At 1.9 miles, turn south on a side road to connect with the Hatfield Ridge Loop to Charit Creek and then ride back along Fork Ridge Road to the Middle Creek Equestrian Trailhead. The Terry Cemetery Road is scheduled to be upgraded, and a trailhead at its end will provide shorter access to the No Business Creek area of the park; eventually there will be a new Black House Creek Trail that parallels Terry Cemetery Road.

15 The **Terry Cemetery Loop** covers 6.1 miles from the end of Terry Cemetery Road, which you can reach once it is improved and a new trailhead established. If you park at the beginning of the road at Three Forks and ride the road to the beginning of the trail, you'll add 10 miles roundtrip to the ride. From Terry Cemetery Road, head down the old Watson Cemetery Road to the river and then south along the river to Parch Corn Creek and then up the creek and the Parch Corn Connector back to Terry Cemetery Road. Some sections may still be unblazed; so make sure you know the way. A proposed additional loop will descend Longfield Branch to No Business Creek and then head upstream to turn and follow an old road back toward Terry Cemetery Road.

16 The **No Business Loop**, also from the east end of Terry Cemetery Road, offers a ride of 7.1 miles. Head north down Longfield Branch to No Business Creek and then down the No Business Trail that follows the creek to the river at Big Island. Turn south along the river and turn up Watson Cemetery Road to get back to Terry Cemetery Road. Again, some sections may be unblazed, so make sure you know your way; the section south along the river may be rerouted or closed at some future date because of erosion problems.

17 From the Peters Mountain Trailhead at the junction of the Peters Mountain

Outdoor Activities

and Laurel Ridge Roads, you can ride a 20-mile **Miller Branch/Stoopin Oak Loop** by heading up Laurel Ridge Road and at Stepping Rock turning south down to Big Island along Miller Branch; south along the river, you'll then turn up Parch Corn Creek and the connector up to Terry Cemetery Road, then head down Longfield Branch to No Business Creek. Ride east for half a mile and turn north along the rocky tread that follows Tackett Creek; the trail becomes the Stoopin Oak Road that leads up to Peters Mountain Road; this will eventually become the Stoopin Oak Trail. Then turn right one mile to get back to Peters Mountain Trailhead. You can shorten this loop to 15.8 miles by turning up Watson Cemetery Road to get to Terry Cemetery Road and not go as far south as Parch Corn Creek. You can also head up No Business Creek from Big Island to Tackett Creek to shorten the loop to 14.5 miles. This is a proposed horse route, so some of the trail is not blazed at this writing; make sure you know the way and have topographic maps with you.

CAMPING

There are two general fee campgrounds in the park. The campsites are first-come, first-served.

The large Bandy Creek Campground with 190 campsites is open year-round. It's located in the Tennessee portion of the park near the Visitor Center north of TN297 on the west side of the river. The facilities include sites with electric and water hookup, tent campsites, and universally accessible sites. The campground has playgrounds, a swimming pool, a sand volleyball court, and restroom/shower houses. Two group camps can be reserved by contacting the Ranger Office at the park headquarters; there are no electrical hookups in the group camps.

The smaller Blue Heron Campground in the Kentucky portion of the park is open April through November. It has 45 sites for tent camping or RVs up to 35 feet; sites have water, and electric hookup is planned for the future. The campground is north of the Mine 18 Road on the way to the Blue Heron Mining Community on the east side of the river. The campground has universally accessible sites, a play structure, and a restroom/shower house.

Exploring the Big South Fork

Camping at the Bandy Creek Campground

Outdoor Activities

Camping at the Big South Fork

Exploring the Big South Fork

In addition to these, there will be three new equestrian camps, each with campsites, bathhouse, and hitching posts. The camps at Station Camp East and near the Bear Creek Scenic Area will open in 1994, and one in the Middle Creek area is scheduled to go in near the equestrian trailhead. These will also be fee campgrounds. Although these camps are designed for camping with horses, nonhorse people may also stay in available spaces if they are willing to camp with horses around.

Alum Ford at the end of KY700 past the Yahoo Falls Scenic Area has primitive camping with 7 sites and pit toilets; no water or electricity and no fee.

Use only down and dead timber for camp fires. Do not use chainsaws to cut firewood.

You may camp virtually anywhere in the backcountry, but set up at least 25 feet from trails, gravel and dirt roads, rock shelters, the gorge rim, and major geologic and historic features, at least 100 feet from streams and the center line of paved roads, 200 feet from parking lots, trailheads, and other developed areas, but only if you will not be visible, and 200 feet from cemeteries and gravesites. If you intend to camp near the river, set up on a high area, because the river can rise rapidly from rain upstream, sometimes many feet in just a few hours.

You will occasionally find specified "no camping" areas, usually designated because an area has become overused. At the various established campgrounds, camping is permitted only at designated sites, except by a special use permit.

Registration for backcountry camping is not required at this time, but it is a good idea to tell someone where you intend to spend the night.

BACKCOUNTRY LODGING

The only lodging within the park is at Charit Creek Lodge in the backcountry, accessible only by hiking and horse trails. Reservations are needed for this concessionaire facility (615/429-5704); the lodge will take people who just walk in if there happens to be room, but don't count on it.

You'll have a special experience at Charit Creek Lodge, staying in the backcountry yet having your basic needs taken care of. The lodge rests in a hollow at the confluence of Charit and Station Camp Creeks. The main lodge building incorporates old log cabins, and the two bunkhouses are also historic log cabins. Hiking and horse trails lead out from the lodge. Charit Creek can also be a base from which to do mountain biking.

At present, the lodge has two bunk rooms and two bunkhouse cabins that each sleep 12 people. If your group has as many as 6 people, you can get a room or bunkhouse to yourselves; otherwise, you will share space with other guests if more than four groups are registered. The lodge has long-range plans to build a few single cabins that can be rented by smaller groups, families, or individuals.

There is no electricity at Charit Creek. The rooms and cabins are heated by woodstoves in winter. At night you'll use kerosene lanterns. You'll wash in a solar-powered bathhouse with propane backup. Bed linens are provided, but you must bring your own towel and washcloth.

Breakfast and dinner are included in the lodging fee. Lunch can also be had by reservation for lodge guests and anyone else who plans on passing through. Up to 12 people at a time may stay at the lodge as hostel guests at a lower rate; you bring your own bedroll and no meals are provided, but you do have use of the kitchen.

Stables with hay are available for lodge guests to board horses overnight. You may also leave a horse out to pasture. There is a fee for both.

The lodge is open year-round, except Christmas and Christmas Eve. Only hostel accommodations are available on Thanksgiving day.

The shortest routes to Charit Creek Lodge lead from the parking area at the end of Fork Ridge Road in the Middle Creek area. Horse riders and mountain bikers can descend the steep road past the gate 1.5 miles to the lodge, while hikers can take the more scenic Charit Creek Lodge Trail 0.8 mile one-way. For longer and more scenic routes, horse riders and mountain bikers can take the horse trails north from Bandy Creek, and hikers can walk the 0.7-mile Twin Arches Trail to Twin Arches and connect with the Twin Arches/Charit Creek Loop where it's 1.1 miles left or 3.5 miles right along the loop to the lodge.

PADDLING

The Big South Fork is rapidly becoming known as one of the major whitewater rivers of the Southeast. About 86 miles of the river and its tributaries flow through the BSFNRRA. Most of the river miles can be paddled either by canoe, kayak, or raft.

This is a free-flowing river for most of its length, and so paddling is seasonal. There are some sections at low water that are suitable for lazy tubing, and others at times of high water that should not be attempted by canoe or raft regardless of a paddler's experience. Between these extremes, the river offers a fun experience ranging from placid sections for beginners to whitewater with Class III and IV rapids and more for the advanced.

If you want to be out more than a day, you may camp next to the river on overnight trips. But always camp high above the river, which has been known to rise many feet overnight from rain upstream.

Motorized boats are permitted only on the section of main channel from the Blue Heron area north; they may operate from 0.1 mile below Devil's Jump Rapids. This section constitutes the upper reaches of Lake Cumberland created by the Wolf Creek Dam far downstream on the Cumberland River.

If you have little experience with paddling whitewater, you should contact one of the local outfitters for a guided trip. At this writing, Cumberland Rapid Transit (615/879-4818) and Sheltowee Trace Outfitters (800/541-RAFT) provide guided raft trips plus canoe rental and shuttle service; Backwoods Adventure (615/569-9573) provides canoe and raft rental and shuttle service. Contact the park Visitor Center for any new outfitters that now also provide guided trips in the area.

If you are experienced or going with friends who are experienced and intend to paddle the river on your own, you'll need to bring your own equipment or rent, study a description of the river in published river guides, arrange for a shuttle to get back to your vehicles, and use commonly recommended safety practices.

Kayaking the river system (Courtesy of the NPS)

Exploring the Big South Fork

Recommended Safety Practices for Paddling

- Plan ahead and let a park ranger know what you are doing.
- Do not attempt a part of the river for which you are not prepared by experience.
- Always wear an approved life jacket and helmet.
- Never boat alone; there should be two other boats in your party to assist if one boat has an accident.
- Notice weather conditions and dress appropriately; wool clothing or a wet suit may be necessary if the weather is cool. Be aware of the dangers of hypothermia, and be prepared to take planned action if one of your group shows the symptoms.
- Scout all major rapids and set up throw ropes before attempting the run. Portage waterfalls, high rapids, and flow-through hazards.
- If your boat capsizes, hold on while getting upstream of the craft. Orient yourself on your back with your feet downstream, toes pointed. Release the boat only if necessary, but stay upstream of the boat so you do not get pinned against a boulder. If you see that you are about to go over a drop or ledge, ball up to keep arms and legs from getting caught in crevices; once you're out of the rapid, resume the position with toes pointed downstream. Never try to stand up in fast water. When you reach a placid section of the river, then you can retrieve your boat and/or get out of the water.
- Carry along dry clothing and a first aid kit in a secured waterproof container. You should also have in your craft a spare paddle, a bailer, extra flotation if in a canoe, and a throw line.
- On the narrower streams, watch for log jams; you may have to portage around.

Always keep in mind that the river is ever changing. Rain upriver can quickly change the water conditions; so always check the weather before taking a river trip. Check with the rangers at the Visitor Center about the current water flow on the day of your trip to ensure the stream is running between the recommended minimum and maximum. The maximum you can handle is, of course, subjective, and for your group, should be based on the skill of your least-experienced member.

Future plans call for the installation of an electronic gauge at Leatherwood Ford that will give the flow in cubic feet per second and the

Top: Information gazebo at Leatherwood Ford
Bottom: River at low water below Leatherwood Ford

Exploring the Big South Fork

air and water temperature. At present, there are staff gauges at the old wooden bridge at Leatherwood Ford and a conversion chart in the gazebo so you can convert from feet to water flow in cubic feet per second; on the conversion chart the y-axis is feet and the x-axis is tenths of feet, both of which you get from your reading of the staff gauges. The lower staff gauge is on the second pier of the bridge, the upper staff gauge stands to the left of the walk down to the bridge, and the middle staff should be between the two but at this writing is missing; it may be reinstalled by the time you read this.

After Visitor Center hours, you can get an estimated flow rate by calling the Army Corp of Engineers (615/736-5455) for a taped message of the Cumberland River system; the Big South Fork is mentioned last. This recorded message, which gives the flow rate of the river at Bear Creek, is updated once in a 24-hour period; the river can change much more quickly than that, so you must also keep in mind the current

Flood stage at Leatherwood Ford

weather conditions. Once you have the flow rate, you can compare the current conditions to the recommended minimums and maximums for the river or tributary sections you intend to paddle in the accompanying chart.

In case of emergencies, telephones are located at Leatherwood Ford and Blue Heron. In addition to designated river access points, there are footpaths for walkout at several places. In the gorge section, you'll find a road at the confluence of the New and Clear Fork Rivers on the right that leads up to the Scott County Airport, a trail at Honey Creek on the left that leads up to the overlook, and a trail at Pine Creek that connects with the O&W Railbed. From Leatherwood Ford to the Station Camp river ford, a trail parallels the river on the right that allows you to get back to Leatherwood Ford to the south or hike to Station Camp Ford to the north. At Station Camp Ford, you can walk up the Station Camp Road on the right or, on the left side of the river, follow a horse trail up to Charit Creek Lodge. Trails parallel both sides of the river from Station Camp Ford to Big Island; about a mile south of Big Island on the east side of the river, you can spend the night at the Burke Cabin up the slope that's also used by horse riders. Farther north, you can walk out at Williams Creek and Bear Creek, both on the right, and at Blue Heron.

In addition to the river access described in the accompanying chart, the Bear Creek Gage Road down from the Bear Creek Scenic Area can be used as river access if you want to carry a canoe or tube a steep half mile down from the gate. You'll find a parking area next to the road 0.3 mile south of the parking for the Bear Creek Overlook.

You can also walk the 0.4-mile trail down to the confluence to put in at that location. At 2.7 miles south of Oneida on US27 turn west on the road to the airport. Cross a bridge over the railroad line and immediately turn left. At 3.8 miles turn right, and then at 4.8 miles turn left onto a gravel road that passes behind the Scott County Memorial Airport. At 7.5 miles keep left with the main graveled road at a fork; the right fork will eventually lead to a proposed Rapids Overlook and trailhead with a trail down to the river. Continuing on the main road, you'll cross the park boundary at 7.9 miles and then reach the end of the road and a loop turnaround and parking at 8.8 miles. The road can get muddy in places after a recent rain, but there is enough gravel a passenger car should be able to make it. From the parking area, walk the gated road to the right, which leads down to the confluence.

River Access on the Big South Fork System

(described south to north moving downstream)

- The **Peters Bridge River Access** at the southern-most boundary of the BSFNRRA provides access to the Clear Fork River, one of the two primary tributary streams that create the Big South Fork. Take TN52 west from Rugby town center 9.5 miles to a left turn on the Peters Ford Road beside the Pleasant View Church of the Nazarene; you'll see a sign for the river access. The bridge is then 4.5 miles along the road.

- The **Rugby River Access** just 2.5 miles west of Rugby town center on TN52 provides additional access to the Clear Fork River. On the far side of the Brewster Bridge (also called Potter Bridge), you'll find a turn to the right that leads down along the river.

- **White Oak Creek Access** just 0.9 mile east of Rugby on TN52 gives access to a primary tributary of the Clear Fork River. There is no sign there; on the west side of the bridge over White Oak Creek make a sharp turn on the north side of the highway down toward the old bridge you'll see below. Then follow a faint footpath that leads under the highway bridge to the water's edge.

- At 10 miles south of Oneida on US27, you can turn west and follow the directions given earlier in the section on Access to the **Burnt Mill Bridge River Access** on the Clear Fork River. This putin/takeout is also accessible by turning north on a side road off TN52 a half mile west of Elgin, or from the west, along the Mt. Helen Road 7.1 miles west of Rugby.

- Just 0.7 mile north of the Burnt Mill Bridge turnoff, US27 crosses the New River, the other main tributary stream creating the Big South Fork; this is the **New River Access**. There is no sign there; on the east side of the bridge on the north side of the highway, turn onto a side road and then make an immediate left on a gravel road that leads down beside the bridge to the water's edge.

Outdoor Activities

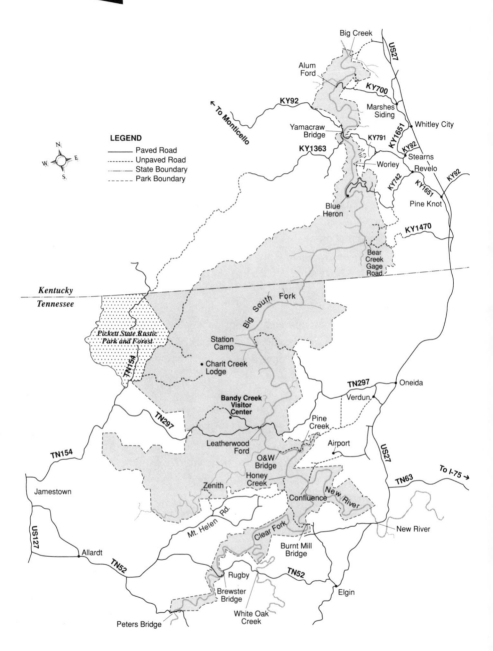

Big Creek

Alum
Ford

KY700

KY92

Marshes
Siding

Whitley City

←To Monticello

Yamacraw
Bridge

KY791

Stearns

KY1363

Worley

Revelo

Pine Knot

KY1470

Blue
Heron

Bear
Creek
Gage
Road

LEGEND

——— Paved Road
········· Unpaved Road
─··─··─ State Boundary
------- Park Boundary

Kentucky

Tennessee

Big South Fork

Pickett State Rustic
Park and Forest

Station
Camp

TN154

• Charit Creek
Lodge

TN297

Oneida

**Bandy Creek
Visitor
Center**

Verdun

TN297

Pine
Creek

TN154

Leatherwood
Ford

Airport

US27

Jamestown

O&W
Bridge

To I-75 →

Honey
Creek

TN63

Zenith

New River

Confluence

US127

Mt. Helen Rd.

New River

Clear Fork

Allardt

Burnt Mill
Bridge

TN52

Rugby

TN52

Elgin

Brewster
Bridge

White Oak
Creek

Peters Bridge

Access to the Big South Fork System

Exploring the Big South Fork

- The **Zenith Access** lies on North White Oak Creek. Zenith was the location of one of the old coal mining camps and coal loading stations that operated along the O&W Railroad. Take TN52 west 7.1 miles from Rugby town center and turn north on Mt. Helen Road (pronounced Hee'-len). In 5.0 miles turn left at a junction, where the old Garrett Store stands, to stay on the Mt. Helen Road and then left again on a gravel road in another 0.3 mile. In another 0.1 mile stay right where a driveway turns left. It's then another 1.1 miles to the creek along a rough road that at this writing is being improved and graveled and should be passable to passenger cars sometime in 1994. The Mt. Helen Road continues on from this turn down to Zenith to connect with the Burnt Mill Ford Road that takes you to the Burnt Mill Bridge River Access in 9 miles. The road becomes graveled when you stay left at a junction at 3 miles to get on the Burnt Mill Ford Road. You'll pass the Honey Creek turnoff at 5 miles.

- There is unofficial river access at **Pine Creek/O&W Bridge** just before Leatherwood Ford. At 1.7 miles west of Oneida on TN297, turn south on Verdun Road. In another 0.6 mile turn right on the O&W Railbed, which becomes graveled in half a mile. It's then 7.6 miles down to the O&W Bridge following the old railroad bed; the O&W stopped operating in 1954 and the tracks were pulled up. The one-lane road crosses five bridges over Pine Creek and is suitable for passenger cars down to the bridge, but not across. You'll see new steps down on the left side of the bridge that provide access to the river. At one mile back up the road, you will have passed on the left a gated side road, which you can walk, that leads steeply down the bluff to a footpath through the woods a quarter mile to the mouth of Pine Creek. Pine Creek is 3 miles before, and O&W Bridge is 2 miles before, Leatherwood Ford; they both provide for alternative takeout and putin. Pine Creek above the putin at its confluence with the river is not runnable and should not be attempted. There is additional access to the O&W Railbed using the Toomey Road; if you're coming from the park headed east on TN297, you'll turn right at the Terry and Terry Store and then in 0.6 mile, turn right off TN297 onto the gravel road. The Toomey Road descends to join the O&W Railbed in 3 miles; the bridge is then 4.2 miles to the right.

- The **Leatherwood Ford River Access** where TN297 crosses the river is the primary takeout/putin on the Big South Fork; follow the directions given earlier in the book to this access point. If you take out at this point, you'll find change stalls and showers near the gazebo.

Bridge support at Worley

Exploring the Big South Fork

- The **Station Camp River Access** at the end of the Station Camp Road is the next takeout/putin north of Leatherwood Ford. Follow the directions given under the section on Access.

- The next river access north is the **Blue Heron River Access** at the end of the Mine 18 Road. Follow the directions given earlier to the Blue Heron Mining Community. At Blue Heron, you'll find change stalls and showers near the river access, which is at the far end of the community.

- The **Worley River Access** is the site of an old mining community and coal loading station on the K&T Railroad. From Stearns, take KY92 west, headed toward the Yamacraw Bridge crossing of the Big South Fork. At 1.8 miles, turn south on KY791; you'll pass through the community of Smith Town. At 1.3 miles along KY791, you'll make a sharp curve right while a side road continues straight. Just after this curve, at 1.4 miles, turn right down a gravel road; at this writing there is no sign marking this turn, so you'll have to watch for it. This steep gravel road leads quickly down toward the river; the condition of the road can deteriorate, so use caution. At 1.7 miles stay to the right as a side road heads up left. At 2.0 miles you must make a hairpin turn; if that poses a problem, stay straight ahead to a turnaround from where you can then head back to the turn, approaching it straight on. Near this turnaround notice the concrete steps leading down the slope from above and below the road; 165 in all, these steps connected a water tank high up on the slope to a water pumping station down on the river when steam engines were used on the K&T Railroad. Continuing down the access road, you'll reach parking near the river at 2.3 miles. The putin/takeout is just ahead. You'll cross the tracks of the K&T that once led down from Stearns for the purpose of hauling timber and coal out of the area. The scenic railway out of Stearns follows the old route of the K&T, but once at the river, it turns south toward Blue Heron instead of north toward Worley. At the river, you'll still see the old concrete supports for a bridge that once spanned the river.

- The next access north is at the **Yamacraw Bridge River Access** on the Big South Fork; follow the directions given earlier in the Access section to the Yamacraw Day Use Area, and on the west side of the river, turn south on KY1363 and immediately turn left down a graveled road to the river's edge; the road is rough at this writing but is scheduled for improvement.

- You can reach the **Alum Ford River Access** and a boat ramp at the end of KY700; follow the directions given earlier for the Yahoo Falls Scenic Area.

Outdoor Activities

• The last access within the park is at **Big Creek** at the very northern tip of the park. From the KY700 turn off US27 for Yahoo Falls and Alum Ford, continue north 3.4 miles on US27; you'll pass the Stearns Ranger District Office of the Daniel Boone National Forest. Turn left on a side road where you'll see a sign for the Sheltowee Trace. Cross railroad tracks and pass a couple of turns to a left turn on a Forest Service road in 0.6 mile from US27. Stay left at a fork, and then at 1.0 mile, when the road seems to curve right and stop, continue straight at the curve onto a gravel road; you'll see a sign for FSR663. Eventually the road will curve left and right as it begins a descent into the Big South Fork Gorge. At 3.0 miles turn right to stay on FSR663 while FSR663A continues straight. After the turn, the road becomes narrow and rocky and could be muddy in places after a recent rain. You'll enter the park boundary and descend steeply to the river and a boat ramp at 3.7 miles.

River Guide to the Big South Fork System

Distance (mi.)	Difficulty (Int. Scale)	Avg. Drop (ft./mi.)	Season	Comments

Peters Bridge to Rugby Access (Brewster Bridge)
(Clear Fork River)

6	I-II	7	W,Sp	short drops, long pools

Rugby Access to Burnt Mill Bridge
(Clear Fork River)

10.5	II-III	12	F,W,Sp	numerous boulders, moderate rapids, water increases below White Oak Cr.

White Oak Creek to Burnt Mill Bridge
(White Oak Creek, Clear Fork River)

11	II	13	W,Sp	no major rapids

Burnt Mill Bridge to Leatherwood Ford
(Clear Fork River, Big South Fork)

11	III-IV	20	F,W,Sp	serious whitewater, Clear Fork joins with New River to create Big South Fork in river Gorge, major rapids—*First Drop, Double Falls, Washing Machine,The Ell, Honey Creek, Rion's Eddy, Jake's Hole, O&W Rapids*

Distance (mi.)	Difficulty (Int. Scale)	Avg. Drop (ft./mi.)	Season	Comments

New River to Leatherwood Ford
(New River, Big South Fork)

15.5	I-IV	14	F,W,Sp	first 6 miles easy on New River but river has silt and mine drainage, II-III ledges before joining with Clear Fork to create Big South Fork, then major rapids—*Double Falls, Washing Machine, The Ell, Honey Creek, Rion's Eddy, Jake's Hole, O&W Rapids*

Zenith to Leatherwood Ford
(North White Oak Creek, Big South Fork)

8.5	II-III	22	W,Sp	short rapids, gradient fluctuates

Leatherwood Ford to Station Camp
(Big South Fork)

8	II-IV	5	F,W,Sp	relatively clear channel, moderate waves, major rapid—*Angel Falls* (portage at 3000 or more cfs)

Station Camp to Blue Heron
(Big South Fork)

19	II-IV	5	F,W,Sp	relatively clear channel, moderate waves, major rapids—*Big Shoals, Devil's Jump* (portage at 3000 or more cfs)

Blue Heron to Worley
(Big South Fork)

2.5	II	5	F,W,Sp	relatively clear channel

Worley to Yamacraw Bridge
(Big South Fork)

2.5	II	5	F,W,Sp	relatively clear channel

Yamacraw Bridge to Alum Ford
(Big South Fork)

5	I-II	5-0	F,W,Sp	clear channel, lake water begins

Outdoor Activities

Distance (mi.)	Difficulty (Int. Scale)	Avg. Drop (ft./mi.)	Season	Comments
Alum Ford to Big Creek (Big South Fork)				
4	I	0	All Year	clear channel, lake water

Recommended Minimum and Maximum Flows

River Section	Minimum	Maximum
Clear Fork before Burnt Mill Bridge :		
Canoes and kayaks	600 cfs	5000 cfs
Rafts	1200 cfs	15,000 cfs
White Oak Creek:		
Canoes and kayaks	1000 cfs	7000 cfs
Rafts	2000 cfs	10,000 cfs
Big South Fork from Burnt Mill Bridge to Leatherwood Ford:		
Canoes and kayaks	600 cfs	3000 cfs
Rafts	1100 cfs	10,000 cfs
New River:		
Canoes and kayaks	600 cfs	5000 cfs
Rafts	1200 cfs	10,000 cfs
North White Oak Creek:		
Canoes and kayaks	1800 cfs	10,000 cfs
Rafts	Too narrow for rafting	
Big South Fork downstream from Leatherwood Ford:		
Canoes and kayaks	150 cfs	3000 cfs
Rafts	400 cfs	15,000 cfs

(minimums represent water needed to paddle the stream; maximums are guidelines on which to base a judgement of your own abilities; numbers based on Leatherwood Ford gauge)

ROAD BICYCLING

All of the highways and back roads open to passenger car traffic are open and suitable for bicycling. Those that are not paved can be rough and do have loose gravel; so you might be better off using a mountain bike or similar type of bicycle with knobby tires on the dirt or gravel roads.

Riding TN297 through the park is quite an experience; the paved road dips into the gorge to Leatherwood Ford and back up. Within the park, TN297 has good shoulders for easy biking. You can park at either the West Entrance Trailhead, or at the beginning of the dirt road to the O&W Overlook that's just inside the East Entrance on the south side of the road, and then ride between these two points for a trip of 7.3 miles one-way. Due to the steepness of the road in and out of the gorge area, you'll need to be in good shape to make the trip. Because of the unrelenting steepness and curving nature of the road down to the river, and because the shoulders get a little narrow in the gorge, it is advisable that you walk your bicycle when descending, or at least make sure you have good brakes.

In the Kentucky portion of the park, you can ride from the town of Stearns on KY1651 south to Revelo where you'll turn right on KY742 and ride down to the Blue Heron Mining Community for a trip of 9.3 miles one-way; there is no shoulder to speak of and some parts are steep, so be careful. You can add a side trip along the way by biking out to the Devil's Jump and Blue Heron Overlooks on the Overlooks Road, which also has no shoulder. If you want to avoid the tough ride back out of the gorge, you can combine a bike ride down to Blue Heron with a train ride back to Stearns on the Big South Fork Scenic Railway; purchase your one-way ticket and check the departure times at the railway office and giftshop in Stearns; get permission to take your bike on the train.

You'll find easier riding if you stay in the rim area and not descend into the river gorge. For example, you can begin at the Bandy Creek Visitor Center in Tennessee and head back out to TN297 and turn west, riding the highway all the way to TN154 and then heading north to the Middle Creek area and Pickett State Rustic Park, 16 miles one-way, or as far as you want to go; TN297 to TN154 has ample shoulders. In

Kentucky, you can ride from Stearns to the Devil's Jump and Blue Heron Overlooks and back for a roundtrip ride of 16.6 miles.

You'll need to keep your bicycle in good shape to handle the ascents and descents. Watch for traffic; some drivers in the region are not yet accustomed to bike riders. Always wear a helmet. Backwoods Adventure in Oneida offers bicycle rental.

MOUNTAIN BIKING

Along with hiking, horseback riding, and river paddling, mountain biking is quickly becoming a major outdoor activity in the BSFNRRA. The park offers some of the best opportunity for biking in the Southeast along old roads, horse trails, and a few routes specifically designed for mountain bikes.

If you have a mountain bike or other bicycle suitable for off-road use, you can ride the Duncan Hollow and Collier Ridge Loop mountain bike trails constructed and maintained by the Big South Fork Bicycle Club. This club of local volunteers is working with the park staff to increase mountain biking opportunities in the park.

In addition to these bike trails, you can also ride many old dirt roads that wind through the park in the adjacent area; if a road is grown up in trees and brush or if it is blazed for hiking, it is not considered an existing road and so is not open to bicycles. While exploring some of the unmarked roads in the park, you'll need to pay attention to where you are; it's easy to get lost. You should get topographic maps of the area you'll be riding in, available at the Visitor Center; many of the old roads appear on the topos.

Mountain bikers may also use the horse trails, but bicycles are not permitted on designated hiking trails; you may not even walk a bicycle down a hiking trail unless it is designated as a multiple-use trail. If you ride the horse trails, you should stop your bike and move to the side any time you encounter horses to allow them to get by. Stand still and speak in a normal voice; do not call out, which would startle the horses. You can get a trail map at the Visitor Center that shows both hiking and horse trails.

Mountain biking at the Big South Fork

Plan your route ahead of time and study the trail and road connections. Ask the rangers about the current conditions of the trails and about any problem areas, such as stream crossings and rock ledges that are difficult to negotiate. You should let the rangers know where you are going, especially if you are exploring old roads; at least let a friend or member of your family know where you intend to be so they can contact the park staff if you get into trouble and do not return when expected. It is best to ride with someone; then if one of you is injured, a person will be there to care for the injured person and to go for help.

Keep your bike in good shape to handle the rough roads and steep ascents and descents. Always wear a helmet. Take plenty of drinking water along or be prepared to purify creek water if you intend to stay in the backcountry for long; water is also available at Bandy Creek, Leatherwood Ford, Charit Creek Lodge, and Blue Heron. If you are camping in the backcountry, you of course must pack along all the necessary equipment for spending the night outside.

Outdoor Activities

Backwoods Adventure offers bicycle rental, and Cumberland Rapid Transit offers guided bike trips. Each summer the park hosts a Mountain Bike Rally that includes the Cumberland Mountain Bike Championship race; contact the Big South Fork Bicycle Club (615/569-4080) for details.

Popular Mountain Bike Routes at the Big South Fork

1   The 5.3-mile **Duncan Hollow Loop** mountain bike trail begins at the Bandy Creek Visitor Center, where you can get a map and description of the two designated mountain bike trails. From the Visitor Center, the trail heads into the campground and takes Duncan Hollow Road north and then turns west on By-Pass Road; the bike trail then leaves the road to loop through the woods and reconnect with By-Pass Road and then return along Duncan Hollow Road; the route is marked with posts that have orange lettering and arrows. A proposed addition will be a John Litton Loop south off Duncan Hollow Road.

2   The 8-mile **Collier Ridge Loop** mountain bike trail also begins at the Bandy Creek Visitor Center; heading west on the Bandy Creek Road past the Clara Sue Blevins Historic Site, the bike trail then turns south off the gravel road to loop through the woods, fording the north and south branches of Bandy Creek and for a time emerging on TN297; a proposed trail section north of TN297 will eventually get you off the highway. This route is also marked with posts that have orange arrows but also white arrows on brown metal signs.

3   There is also a 1.5-mile **West Bandy Creek Trail** off the Bandy Creek Road that has been used in bike races; this trail is often narrow and steep and not for beginners. Ride down the road 2.7 miles from the Visitor Center or 0.6 mile in from the West Entrance and watch for the trail on the north side of the road; the trail circles east to come out one mile back along the Bandy Creek Road toward the Visitor Center. The trail is flagged with blue strips, which will probably be replaced with more permanent signs soon. Watch for the flags through several turns—left on an old road then right; later, right on a road then left; left on a road (that leads to the right out to Bandy Creek Road if you want to cut the ride short) and after a 100 yards a turn right off the road; after dropping steeply to a creek, turn right up a road and swing left; toward the end, join another road and go right;

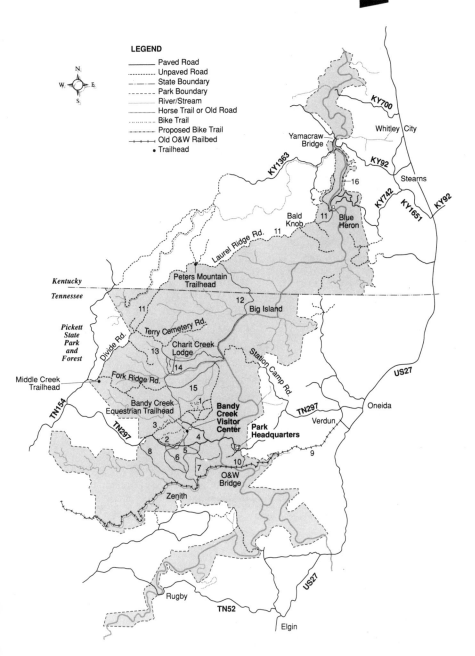

LEGEND

Paved Road
Unpaved Road
State Boundary
Park Boundary
River/Stream
Horse Trail or Old Road
Bike Trail
Proposed Bike Trail
Old O&W Railbed
• Trailhead

Mountain Bike Trails of the Big South Fork

Outdoor Activities

then another road and go right out to Bandy Creek Road. At the last road junction, you can turn left to add an even more difficult section, definitely not for beginners; the trail drops steeply to a cross a small creek and then up to a road and turn right; in a more open area turn right off the road; cross two more small creeks; make a left turn; and then join another road and go right out to Bandy Creek Road.

4   If you are a beginner to mountain biking, you may want to first try the loop formed by the **Bandy Creek Road and TN297**; part of the route is over a gravel road and so gives you some experience riding unpaved track. Start from the Visitor Center and head west on Bandy Creek Road; in 0.2 mile it becomes gravel, and you'll then have a 3.1-mile ride on unpaved road to TN297 at the West Entrance Trailhead. Then turn east on TN297 and ride back to the Bandy Creek Road and the Visitor Center for a loop ride of 9 miles.

5   From the Bandy Creek area, you can also ride the 18.5-mile **North White Oak Loop**, starting at the Bandy Creek Equestrian Trailhead. This is one of the popular routes for bicycles that use horse trails, although it has been mentioned that bicycles might not be allowed on this trail in the future; so check with the Visitor Center. This route passes by a 2.3-mile side trip to an overlook of Leatherwood Ford. If you only ride the loop section and include the 1.6-mile side trail to the North White Oak Creek Overlook, you'll have a ride of 21.7 miles. If you only ride to the Leatherwood Overlook, it's a ride of 10.4 miles roundtrip. Check the horse trail description for details.

6   You can also ride the **Gar Blevins Trail** which follows the old Gar Blevins Road that cuts through the middle of the North White Oak Loop for about a 7-mile roundtrip ride to North White Oak Creek Overlook and back. Stay left at the fork. The road begins south off TN297 one mile east of the West Entrance or 3 miles west of the east end of Bandy Creek Road; the first several yards are paved, and you may park there, but stay to the side so as not to block access to the trail. This also has been mentioned to be closed to bicycles, so check with the Visitor Center.

7   On TN297, you can also take the **Coyle Branch Trail** south along the old Coyle Branch Road toward North White Oak Creek and descend to the old O&W Railroad bed in about 5 miles; be aware the descent is rough and rocky. Before the descent, the road for a time coincides with the North White Oak Loop, and

you'll pass the side trail that leads to the Leatherwood Overlook. There are two access points for this road on TN297. One just west of the White Pine Church, 0.6 mile west of the Bandy Creek Road, is a rough track that fords Bandy Creek; the "Road Ends" sign just refers to motorized traffic. The second access is 1.2 miles west of the Bandy Creek Road; it heads south to quickly intersect with the North White Oak Loop, where you'll turn left; you can, of course, begin the North White Oak Loop at this location. You'll see at both access points a paved section of a few yards before the trail leads into the woods; you may park at these two locations, but again stay to the side.

8 You can also reach the O&W Railbed along the 6-mile **Gernt Trail** that begins as a small road track on the east side of the Hitching Post Grocery that's 1 mile outside the west park boundary; the store is operated by one of the Slaven family. Following the Gernt Road, the trail reenters the park and heads south toward North White Oak Creek, descending to the railbed at the site of the old community of Gernt, which was a mining and lumber camp along the O&W where the Gernt family, German settlers in the region, had interests. Watch for a good overlook at the start of the descent. Again, this is a tough descent, rocky and rough.

9 The old **O&W Railbed** itself is fun for mountain biking. You can ride the gravel road that now follows the railbed down from Verdun 8.2 miles to the O&W Bridge; check the directions given in the section on paddling. It's a great ride that crosses five bridges over Pine Creek and passes between rock walls; you should walk your bikes over the bridges because there are gaps in the planking that can catch a tire. Keep in mind that at least for the present this road is maintained by the county for vehicular traffic. It is also a popular route for four-wheel driving—not too bad during the week, but on weekends you could be eating a lot of dust. (Several studies have recommended that the road be converted to a hiking/bicycling trail within the park; so at some future time, the road at the boundary of the park, or closer to the river, may be closed and used only for hiking and bicycling.) Once you are down to the river, you can walk your bike across the O&W Bridge and continue riding on the old railbed about a mile to a ford of North White Oak Creek; here you'll leave most traffic behind and enjoy more solitude along 6 miles of the old railbed to Zenith, passing the Coyle Branch Road and the Gernt Road along the way; the route is likely to have many long, deep mudholes, which makes it even more fun. If you intend to come out at Zenith, you must ford the creek again and follow the gravel road up to the Mt.

Helen Road; check the section on paddling for directions. The railbed from Zenith on becomes overgrown, but you can probably make it as far as Mill Seat Creek.

10 There's also a 2-mile roundtrip ride out to the **O&W Overlook** along a dirt road on the south side of TN297; the road begins just inside the park from the east entrance sign. At the overlook, from the top of a bluff called "Yellow Cliffs," you'll have a panoramic view that includes the O&W Railroad Bridge over the Big South Fork. Be careful; there are no railings at the overlook. A proposed East Rim Trail for mountain bikes will connect O&W Overlook with Sunset Overlook and the East Rim Overlook Road.

11 From the Middle Creek Trailhead on the west side of the park, you can ride Divide Road, joining the **Long Trail** for horses, into the Kentucky portion of the park (Divide Road becomes the Peters Mountain Road at the state line) and then taking Laurel Ridge Road, following the horse-head blaze through a couple of turns, to Bald Knob and then turn down the Waters Cemetery Road and follow the horse trail northeast to Blue Heron, a ride of about 23 miles; check the horse trail description for details. For bicycles to avoid the ford of the river on the horse trail, it has been proposed that the hiking trail leading to the tram bridge at Blue Heron be designated multiple use and that you be allowed to walk your bike across the bridge; check with the park rangers for whether that change has been made. Once you get to Blue Heron, you'll need a shuttle to pick you up, unless you intend to ride back. The shuttle can meet you in Stearns if you want to ride the Big South Fork Scenic Railway one-way out of Blue Heron.

12 You can make a loop of 30 miles on the **Big Island Branch Loop** off the Long Trail by turning off Laurel Ridge Road at Stepping Rock and following the horse trail down to Big Island and on to Station Camp Creek and up the creek to Charit Creek Lodge and then along Fork Ridge Road back to Divide Road and the Middle Creek Trailhead; check the horse trail description. Be aware that the portion of the loop along the river is soft and sandy and used frequently by horses, and so you'll often be pushing your bike and standing aside. That section of the horse trail is scheduled to be rerouted at some future time. You might want to do this in winter when there is less horse traffic.

13 The **Hatfield Ridge Branch Loop** off the Long Trail forms a 14.4-mile circuit by turning south off Divide Road at Three Forks on the Terry Cemetery

Road, then at 1.9 miles, turning south on a side road that's also a horse trail to connect with the Hatfield Ridge Loop to Charit Creek. You can then ride back along Fork Ridge Road to Divide Road and the Middle Creek Trailhead.

14   From Charit Creek Lodge, you can ride the 9.9-mile **Hatfield Ridge Loop**, which is a horse trail, first following the Station Camp Creek Trail toward the Big South Fork, fording the creek several times, and then turning up Hatfield Ridge to circle back to the lodge with views along the way, including a side trail to the Charit Creek Overlook.

15   Or from the lodge, you can ride the **Station Camp Creek Trail, Duncan Hollow Trail,** and **Charit Creek Horse Trail** combined for a 12.7-mile loop ride to Bandy Creek and back. You can, of course, also start at the Bandy Creek Visitor Center and ride to Charit Creek Lodge and back. Be aware there are a number of crossings of Station Camp Creek; you can avoid the crossings by riding up the Charit Creek Horse Trail 1.5 miles from the lodge and taking the Fork Ridge Trail east to connect with the Duncan Hollow Trail.

16   A proposed 9-mile **Yamacraw Loop** mountain bike trail will begin at the Blue Heron Mining Community and head north along the river, following the old railbed of the K&T; the trail will pass through the site of Worley and continue on to cross the river to the west side on the old K&T bridge at Yamacraw. The trail will then head south along Wilson Ridge Road to connect with the Kentucky Trail and follow it down to the tram bridge at Blue Heron where you'll walk your bike across the bridge to reenter the mining community. It may be some time yet before the trail is approved and constructed, but watch for it.

CLIMBING AND RAPPELLING

The BSFNRRA with its walls of sandstone offers exciting opportunities for rock climbing and rappelling. But remember these are inherently dangerous activities; you should be experienced or be with someone who is experienced before climbing or rappelling in the park. The park has no officially designated places for this activity.

A popular place for climbing and rappelling is the O&W Overlook, which you reach by walking or driving the mile-long four-wheel drive dirt

Outdoor Activities

Rappelling at the Big South Fork (Courtesy of the NPS)

road to the south off TN297 just inside the East Entrance to the park. But the rock wall there is quite high and intimidating. So you might want to stay with shorter rock walls that you'll find virtually everywhere in the park.

In Kentucky, on the Mine 18 Road down to Blue Heron, just after the road curves left where there has been some construction work to stabilize the road, a good rock wall stands up the slope to the left of the road; watch for a parking area on the left after the rock wall where you can park and walk back up the road. The Twin Arches/Charit Creek Loop offers a variety of climbs on the section of trail from Twin Arches counterclockwise toward Jake's Place where it passes along a rock wall. If you want to hike into the backcountry to climb, you'll find good rock in the No Business Creek area.

You should not climb at developed overlooks or any other high-use areas where you might endanger other visitors. Climbing on Twin Arches, Yahoo Falls, or any other geologic formation is not permitted to prevent damage to these structures and to protect the scenic values for other visitors. You are not permitted to damage a rock face in any way; so you may not drive climbing nails or spikes into the rock walls. Other regulations and recommendations may apply when the park staff completes a climbing management plan that is being worked on; check with the park rangers.

Always climb with others and let someone else know where you are and what you are doing, just in case of accident; filing a plan with the rangers is always a good idea. You should have all the proper climbing and safety equipment. Cumberland Rapid Transit offers rock climbing and rappelling instruction.

CAVING

The BSFNRRA abounds in rock shelters where light penetrates all the way to the back of the openings. These can be explored by anyone agile enough to scramble through boulders, but use caution. Do not dig for artifacts under the rock shelters, such artifacts are protected by federal law. You may not camp or start fires in the shelters.

The park lacks true caves because the rock is sandstone. The river has only just eroded down to limestone, the rock in which deep caves are formed. Station Camp, Parch Corn, and No Business Creeks have reached the limestone in their lower portions where they meet the river, and so perhaps there are caves in that region, but none have been recorded. If you do find a cave, you should explore it only if you are an experienced spelunker, or going with someone who is experienced, and have all the necessary caving and safety equipment. Report the location of any cave you find to the park's rangers; you must also obtain a permit before entering a cave. Always cave with others and let someone else know where you are and what you are doing in case of accident. Cumberland Rapid Transit offers wild cave tours outside of the park area.

Most abandoned coal mines in the park have been closed or gated. If you happen upon one that is open, do not enter because of the unstable nature of mines and because of dangerous gases that may collect in a mine. Report any open mine to the park rangers.

SWIMMING AND SNORKELING

You'll find a swimming pool at the Bandy Creek Campground. In addition, there are a number of spots in the Big South Fork and its tributary creeks where you can wade and swim at low water, although there are no places specifically designated for swimming in the river system.

The Leatherwood Ford River Access is a fine place for splashing around. You'll find nearby changing stalls and showers for river users. Other traditional places to swim are the Burnt Mill Bridge, Rugby, and Peters Bridge river access points on the Clear Fork River, the Gentlemen's Swimming Hole at Rugby, and the Station Camp and Blue Heron river access points.

At low water when the river runs clear, you can also have fun snorkeling while looking for the various fish and mollusk species that inhabit the river system. The pools around Leatherwood Ford and Blue Heron are suitable for snorkeling.

You should only swim in the river and creeks at low water. Even then, you should be careful; the river possesses deep pools and strong currents; drownings are possible and have occurred. Holes, rocks, undercurrents, and ledges can make you fall and perhaps entrap feet and legs. You should not swim above rapids, where you might get caught in the current and pulled into the rapids. Never swim alone, and never enter the river or streams at high water when you will be unable to fight the current. You swim in the river and creeks at your own risk.

PICNICKING

The park contains 14 developed picnic areas with tables and grills. Restrooms are available at Bandy Creek, Leatherwood Ford, and Blue

Wading in Station Camp Creek

Outdoor Activities

Heron; other sites usually have chemical toilets for use spring, summer, and fall.

Designated Picnic Areas at the Big South Fork

Bandy Creek Visitor Center
Leatherwood Ford River Access
Station Camp River Access
Twin Arches Trailhead
Rugby River Access
Gentlemen's Swimming Hole Trailhead
Burnt Mill Bridge River Access

Honey Creek Overlook
Peters Bridge River Access
Blue Heron Mining Community
Bear Creek Scenic Area
Yamacraw Day Use Area
Yahoo Falls Scenic Area
Alum Ford River Access

Picnicking at the Big South Fork

Directions are given in earlier sections of this book to these locations. One area not listed is quite primitive, the Joe Branch Picnic Area; look for the directions in the section on four-wheel driving. The unmaintained road into Joe Branch is steep and rutted in places and only passable to four-wheel drive until the road is improved. Trails are proposed for the Joe Branch area with a trailhead at the picnic area.

There is also a picnic table at the White Oak Creek River Access, just west of the bridge over White Oak Creek outside the park. Watch for other picnic areas to be established as road access is improved into other areas of the park.

In addition to developed areas, you'll find picturesque locations on the river and shaded streams that are ideal for picnicking. Huge boulders at streamside make excellent spots for laying out a lunch. Make sure you carry out all trash. Be careful near the water and keep an eye on children; falling in the water can mean loss of life at such places as Angel Falls where swift water sweeps past undercut boulders. Watch for snakes that may be lying on rocks in the sun.

SIGHTSEEING

If you want a leisurely visit to the park, there's plenty of opportunity for just sightseeing. Stop by the Bandy Creek Visitor Center for orientation and information and perhaps walk the mile-long nature trail that takes you through an upland forest.

The drive down to Leatherwood Ford on TN297 and a stroll along the river boardwalks lets you experience the river in the Tennessee portion of the park. A visit to the Blue Heron Mining Community in Kentucky along KY742 and Mine 18 Road offers a step back in time to the days of coal mining along the Big South Fork.

If you are interested in the history of the region, you can also hike some of the short trails mentioned in the section on the people of the Big South Fork. And you can drive beyond the Bandy Creek Visitor Center to reach the Clara Sue Blevins Historic Site and the Katie Blevins Cemetery also described in the history section.

Sunset Overlook

You can also take relatively easy short walks to the waterfalls, arches, and rock shelters described in the geology section of this book.

Then there are the various park overlooks that give you an opportunity to get wide-ranging views of the river gorge. In the geology section, you are directed to the Devil's Jump Overlook in the Kentucky portion of the park and to the Honey Creek Overlook in Tennessee to study the creation of the Big South Fork Gorge. Others include the Blue Heron, Bear Creek, and East Rim Overlooks. Some undeveloped overlooks, like the Sunset, O&W, and Angel Falls Overlooks, require some walking; there are many other overlooks not mentioned in the accompanying chart that you'll discover while hiking or riding in the backcountry. Most of those do not have railings, so use caution. Watch for access to be established to such new overlooks as Station Camp East accessible by a proposed trail out of the Station Camp East Trailhead, Maud's Crack you will reach by a proposed trail from the end of Terry Cemetery Road, the Confluence and the Rapids off the road

Exploring the Big South Fork

that runs behind the Scott County Memorial Airport described in the section on paddling, and Hutts Branch off the trail connecting the John Muir Trail with the Kentucky Trail in the No Business Creek area.

Scenic Overlooks at the Big South Fork

Overlook	View/Directions
Devil's Jump	BSF Gorge and Devil's Jump Rapids; take the Overlooks Rd. off the Mine 18 Rd. on the way to Blue Heron.
Blue Heron	BSF Gorge in the vicinity of Blue Heron, but cannot see the Blue Heron Community; continue on the Overlooks Rd. from the Devil's Jump Overlook to the road's end, and then walk the paved trail to the gorge rim.
Catawba	BSF Gorge from the west and Blue Heron Community in the distance; at the Blue Heron Mining Community, walk across the river on the tram bridge and turn south on the hiking trail 1.6 miles to the overlook on the left.
Beech Grove	Blue Heron Mining Community across the river; this overlook is scheduled to be built soon and may be accessible by the time you read this; follow the directions given earlier to the old Beaty oil well, but before Bald Knob Road and just after the Beech Grove Baptist Church, turn left down the Waters Cemetery Road and in 0.3 mile turn left on a new road that will be constructed to lead out to the overlook.
Blue Heron Tipple (undev.)	The tipple and tram bridge over the river; from the mining community, hike the Blue Heron Loop counterclockwise 0.7 mile to where the main trail turns right and an unofficial side trail leads left to the view; or you can reach this point on the loop by taking the side trail from the developed Blue Heron Overlook that drops down to the Blue Heron Loop and then turn right on the loop for 0.2 mile.

Outdoor Activities

Overlook	View/Directions
Bear Creek	Meandering BSF; as KY742 becomes Mine 18 Rd., turn south toward the Bear Creek Scenic Area and follow signs 3.5 miles to the overlook parking and then walk the graveled trail to the overlook.
Split Bow Arch	An arch formed by joint widening and headward erosion; you'll see the overlook to the right as you enter the Bear Creek Scenic Area 0.2 mile before the Bear Creek Overlook parking.
Lake Cumberland	Waters of the lake backed up into the BSF Gorge; from the Yahoo Falls Scenic Area trailhead, walk down the road a short distance and turn right down some steps to the overlook.
Yahoo Creek	The confluence of the creek with the BSF; from the Yahoo Falls Trailhead, walk the Topside Loop a short distance to a side path on the left that leads down to the overlook.
Yahoo Falls	The 113-foot waterfall; continue on the Topside Loop for 0.2 mile to the overlook on the left; you can then continue on the loop to cross the creek above the falls and reach a similar overlook on the other side of the waterfall.
Buzzard Rock (undeveloped)	One of the best views of the Big South Fork Gorge, with the waters of Lake Cumberland; follow the directions given earlier toward the river access at Big Creek in the section on paddling. Then on FSR663, 2.4 miles from US27, watch for a dirt road to the right. Unless you have four-wheel drive and plenty of clearance, park somewhere here so that you do not block the road; it's probably not wise to try to drive through the large mudhole, but you can go around to find space for parking off the road. Then walk up the road for half a mile to its end, staying with the main road where side roads take off. At the end follow the footpath down to Buzzard Rock, a bare rock promontory that has an expansive view.

Overlook	View/Directions
Honey Creek	Bare rock walls and the BSF Gorge; from the Burnt Mill River Access, continue on the Burnt Mill Ford Road 3.4 miles and turn right to reach the overlook in 0.8 mile.
O&W (undeveloped)	BSF Gorge and the O&W Railroad Bridge; just inside the park's East Entrance, follow a four-wheel drive road left 1.1 miles to the gorge rim.
East Rim	BSF Gorge; turn left off TN297 0.5 mile inside the park's East Entrance, drive to end of the road, and walk down to the overlook.
Sunset (undeveloped)	BSF Gorge and confluence of North White Oak Creek; park at the East Rim Trailhead on the road to the East Rim Overlook, and walk south on the Sunset Overlook Trail 1.3 miles to the edge of the gorge.
Leatherwood Ford Bridge	BSF Gorge and the bridge at Leatherwood Ford; from the East Rim Trailhead walk the Leatherwood Ford Loop clockwise 0.4 mile to a 0.1-mile side trail that leads to the overlook.
N. White Oak Creek	Gorge of the BSF tributary where the O&W Railroad once operated; hike, horse ride, or bike the 18.5-mile North White Oak Loop from the Bandy Creek Equestrian Trailhead, or from access on TN297, to about halfway along the loop; or you can follow the Gar Blevins Road 3.5 miles one way through the middle of the loop.
Leatherwood	BSF Gorge and Leatherwood Ford; take a 2.3-mile side trail off the North White Oak Loop east to the overlook.

Outdoor Activities

Overlook	View/Directions
Angel Falls (undeveloped)	Probably the best view in the park of the BSF Gorge; from Leatherwood Ford, hike the John Muir Trail north on the west side of the river 3 miles to turn right on the Grand Gap Loop to reach the view.
Grand Gap Loop (undev.)	Distant view of the Angel Falls Rapids; hike the Grand Gap Loop counterclockwise 1 mile from the junction with the John Muir Trail to where you switchback down to the gorge rim for a short side path to the view.
John Muir (undeveloped)	No Business Creek Valley; backpack the John Muir Trail 26 miles north from Leatherwood Ford into the backcountry, or for a shorter walk of 7 miles, hike east on the John Muir Trail from its crossing of Divide Road in the Middle Creek area.
Charit Creek	Charit Creek Lodge; hike, bike, or horse ride the Hatfield Loop Trail clockwise 1 mile to a half-mile side trail south to the overlook.

PHOTOGRAPHY

The Big South Fork region possesses a geologic landscape that must be photographed. Dramatic scenes include the river gorge, waterfalls, arches, chimneys, and rock shelters. You'll also find old log cabins and barns, weathered gravestones, and railroad bridges that span the rivers and streams.

The best times to photograph are the early mornings and late afternoons with their soft light and long shadows that give a sense of depth to your pictures. Some of the easily accessible gorge overlooks, such as the East Rim and Bear Creek Overlooks, face west, so you'll probably want to visit those in the mornings unless you want a shot of sunset over the gorge. The Devil's Jump and Blue Heron Overlooks face south.

Getting the right picture

The middle part of the day, when the most light penetrates to the forest floor, is perhaps the best time for photographing the more subtle beauties of the park—wildflowers and wildlife, light on water, patterns in the rocks, leaves, and trees.

Those who can take advantage of the opportunities for photography range from the beginner with a simple camera who can't miss with an overlook shot to the professional or experienced amateur who captures a flitting bird or the soft steps of a cascading stream. Even the casual visitor will bring home pictures to show friends and perhaps display on a wall.

When stepping off a trail to take a photograph, leave as little impact as possible. Avoid trampling wildflowers and ferns or causing erosion on a steep bank while getting to your perfect picture.

FOUR-WHEEL DRIVE, ATV, AND TRAIL BIKE RIDING

The BSFNRRA has many miles of dirt roads that provide opportunities for four-wheel drive, all-terrain vehicle, and trail bike riding. This activity is generally limited to unmaintained roads within the adjacent rim area; if a road is grown up in trees and brush or if it is blazed for hiking or mountain biking, it is not considered an existing road and so is not open to vehicular traffic. Such vehicles are not allowed in the gorge area with the current exceptions for licensed vehicles of the Station Camp Road, the Zenith Road, the Burnt Mill Bridge Road, and the O&W Railbed; some of these roads are to be upgraded and so may become restricted, so check with the Visitor Center or a park ranger before going.

You must be at least 16 years of age to drive any motorized vehicle in the park.

Vehicles that are not licensed for highway use are restricted from using publicly maintained roads and highways within the park, including county roads that may appear to be just old dirt roads. Unlicensed vehicles in Tennessee must have a Tennessee Department of Revenue sticker on the vehicle; this sticker is available from any Tennessee

County Clerk. Such stickers are not required for Kentucky vehicles at this time. Operators from outside Tennessee should carry registration or ownership documentation. Such vehicles are required to have headlights and taillights in use from a half hour after sunset to a half hour before sunrise.

While traveling an unmaintained road in the park, do not go beyond any gate, post, berm, or cable intended to restrict access. To protect the environment, travel is restricted to existing roads—do not turn off into any open wildlife plot or agricultural field and do not attempt to blaze a trail through the forest. Do not turn off on any hiking, horseback, or bicycling trail designated solely for such use. Act responsibly and safely while respecting the rights of others to use the park undisturbed. In all cases of encountering horse riders on the roads, pull to the side and stop to not scare the horses and to allow them to get by.

As with any outdoor activity, plan ahead. Obtain the topographical maps that cover the area of your intended trip; these maps show many of the old roads and are available at the Visitor Center. Let the rangers or a friend or family member know where you are going and when you expect to return. Take along a first-aid kit in case of injury, water and food, any equipment you need if spending the night, and a spare ignition key.

It's always best to ride with other vehicles. But leave plenty of space between vehicles in a line.

Always wear a helmet and other protective clothing when riding a trail bike or other unprotected vehicle; Kentucky law requires helmets; Tennessee law requires helmets on public thoroughfares. Make sure you take along tools for repairs so you won't be stranded with a breakdown.

Four-wheel drive vehicles should be equipped with a fire extinguisher, a CB radio, a tow strap, a winch, jumper cables, a shovel or some other trenching tool, repair tools, a jack and tire iron, a slab of wood to form a base for the jack in loose sand or dirt, and of course, a spare tire. Your vehicle should have a seat belt; wear it.

Maintain your vehicle according to the manufacturer's suggested schedule to help avoid breakdowns in the backcountry. Change your air filter after driving dusty roads. Make sure your tires have plenty of tread.

Outdoor Activities

In the backcountry, do not use excessive speed; unless posted otherwise, the speed limit is 25 mph. Approach intersections with caution since there are no stop signs either way. If you want to pass someone, make sure they understand what you intend to do before trying to pull around. If you are being passed, pull over as much as you can to give space to the passer, but not so far that you destroy vegetation beside the road.

Vehicles driving uphill traditionally have the right-of-way. If you're headed downhill on a one lane road and someone is coming uphill, pull over and let them pass without their vehicle having to lose momentum.

Drugs and alcohol have no place with trail bikes or four-wheel driving. Driving under the influence is just as dangerous in the backcountry as it is on city streets.

Some routes that are good for licensed vehicles are the 5.1-mile Terry Cemetery Road east off Divide Road in the Middle Creek area at Three Forks (this road is scheduled to be improved and so will also be open to passenger cars); the rough four-wheel drive Laurel Ridge Road that leads 9 miles from Peters Mountain Trailhead northeast to Bald Knob (the road becomes improved near Bald Knob and leads out to KY1363 in another 5 miles; that stretch is called the Beech Grove/Devils Creek Road; the entire length may be improved at some future time), the 4-mile Duncan Hollow Road north from the Bandy Creek area (also open to passenger car traffic; there are no connections, so you'll have to backtrack), the 17-mile O&W Railbed that leads down from Verdun to cross the bridge, ford North White Oak Creek, and continue on to the Zenith area where you'll ford the creek once again to ascend to the Mt. Helen Road (cross the bridge at your own risk; this route is likely to be closed to motorized traffic at some future time), and the Burnt Mill Ford Road that leads from the Burnt Mill Bridge River Access northwest to a side road north to the Honey Creek Overlook and then continues west to become the paved Mt. Helen Road where you can turn down to the Zenith River Access for a drive of 11 miles one-way including a side trip to Honey Creek Overlook (to the Honey Creek Overlook and back is a roundtrip of 8.6 miles; also open to passenger car traffic).

At this writing it takes four-wheel drive to cover the 2.4-mile Joe Branch Road into the Joe Branch Picnic Area. At 1.9 miles west of the

Honey Creek turnoff on the Burnt Mill Ford Road, turn left when the road becomes the paved Mt. Helen Road. At 2.8 miles from that turn, the road passes the Mt. Helen United Baptist Church and curves sharply to the right where you'll see the beginning of the gravel road on the left into the picnic area. From the west, you can get to this point by turning north off TN52 on the Mt. Helen Road 5 miles to a junction at the old Garrett Store and then bear right as the Mt. Helen Road continues left; from this junction, it's 1.6 miles to the Joe Branch Road. As you head down the road, you'll pass the Mt. Helen Cemetery and then at a fork stay right and then straight where a side road leads to the right. Halfway along the road, curve sharply right as the trace of the old road continues straight a short distance. When you arrive at the picnic area, you'll see a picnic table and grill and a road to the right that leads past another dirt road to the right and then a couple more tables and grills; you can continue down the hill, probably overgrown at this point, to a pond with bluegill and smallmouth bass. Bring along a picnic lunch and a fishing pole and spend some leisure time in the area before returning.

Most other old roads in the park are short one-way roads that provide hunting and fishing access into the backcountry; you may ride these to their end and back just to explore. Unlicensed vehicles may use old fire and logging roads. Popular areas for driving are Williams Creek, Hurricane Ridge, New River, Darrow Ridge, Wilson Ridge, and Yamacraw.

The park staff intends at some future time to designate routes and trails specifically for off-road motor vehicles. ATV areas have been proposed for the southern and northern portions of the park. Check with the Visitor Center for new routes or for other suggestions of old roads to travel.

HUNTING

Hunting is allowed in the BSFNRRA with valid state licenses and subject to state and federal regulations. Keep in mind that the park is in two states; you must have a license for the state in which you are hunting. Licenses are available at local sporting goods and supply stores, many local department stores that have sporting goods sections, county court clerks, and the state fish and wildlife agencies.

Also be aware the seasons vary; while there may be hunting in the Tennessee portion of the park, there may be no hunting in the Kentucky portion, or vice versa. Check with the Kentucky Department of Fish & Wildlife (502/564-4336) and the Tennessee Wildlife Resources Agency (800/262-6704) for the seasons, species limits, and state regulations.

You should check with the park rangers for any federal regulations that apply, especially for the transport of guns. While traveling around the park, your gun must be stored unloaded in your vehicle and in a condition that prevents it from being easily used; for example, with a trigger lock or partial disassembly. You may carry a gun in the field only during designated hunting seasons, and you may fire only at legal game. The gun may be discharged only when taking wildlife during a hunting season; target practice and sighting are not allowed within the park.

The park staff has encouraged wildlife populations through restocking of turkey and an agricultural leasing program and agreement with the Kentucky Department of Wildlife Resources to maintain open fields. Deer were gone by 1915 but were restocked in the 1950s.

Any hunter knows the difficulty in trying to predict where game animals will be; animals move due to environmental stresses and the frequent presence of humans. So you should scout the area for signs of wildlife and ranging animals prior to the actual hunt to improve your chance of success. The No Business Creek-Rock Creek backcountry has the best deer-hunter success ratio in the region, but that simply could be because more people hunt this area. The region west of Bandy Creek also seems to be frequented by deer. The ridge at the end of Duncan Hollow Road and the No Business Creek area are good for wild boar. Grouse and turkey frequent areas of good cover, typically at the edge of fields and where berries are found. Other game animals include quail, dove, squirrel, rabbit, raccoon, and opossum. Black bear is being studied for reintroduction and may not be hunted at this time; in Kentucky, state law prohibits hunting bear.

Vertical yellow "Safety Zone" signs designate the boundary of areas where no hunting is allowed. These exist around the Bandy Creek Campground and Visitor Center, the Oscar Blevins Farm, the East Rim Complex, Charit Creek Lodge, Blue Heron Campground and the Mining Community, Alum Ford, Yahoo Falls Scenic Area, Yamacraw Day Use Area, Worley River Access, Station Camp River Access, Leatherwood Ford River Access, Burnt Mill Bridge River Access, Zenith Access, Rugby River Access, and Peters Bridge River Access.

Portable stands may be used when hunting, but no permanent structures may be attached to trees. Bait or mineral licks may not be used to lure wildlife. Spotlighting is not allowed. Hunting dogs are permitted in the park in conformance with state law; in both states, the dogs must be physically restrained during certain portions of the year; check with the state wildlife agencies for those dates. Tramming, allowing dogs to run ahead of vehicles, is prohibited on Leatherwood Ford Road (TN297), Bandy Creek Road, Blue Heron Road, and Alum Ford Road. You may not hang a carcass in a campground.

Remember that others are also permitted to use the park during hunting season. So be on the lookout for backcountry hikers, mountain bikers, and horseback riders. To avoid contact with nonhunters, keep to the backcountry where fewer people go, and even then it's a good idea to stay 200 feet away from backcountry trails. Always wear blaze orange during hunting season.

FISHING

Fishing is a popular activity in the BSFNRRA; as long ago as the 1880s, sportsmen came from Louisville and Cincinnati to the region to fish. You'll find plenty of bass, bluegill, catfish, walleye, and other game species in the river and its tributary streams, even in the New River,

Fishing at Leatherwood Ford

which still remains polluted with coal mine drainage from outside the park.

Fishing in the park is subject to state and federal regulations. You must have valid state licenses. Keep in mind that the park resides in two states; you must have a license for the state in which you are fishing. Commercial fishing is not allowed.

Licenses are available at local sporting goods and supply stores, many local department stores that have sporting goods sections, county court clerks, and the state fish and wildlife agencies. Check with the Kentucky Department of Fish & Wildlife and the Tennessee Wildlife Resources Agency for creel and size limits and other state regulations.

Leatherwood Ford is one of the popular fishing spots; there's a large pool just upstream of the old wooden bridge. Also, you can cross the old bridge at Leatherwood Ford to the west side of the river and head upstream along a footpath a few hundred yards to the mouth of Bandy Creek where you'll find a nice fishing hole in the river; this footpath is not an official trail and gets quite overgrown in summer. An easier route follows the John Muir Trail south from Leatherwood Ford on the east side of the river, past the end of the universally accessible part, to where the trail dips into a drainage at 0.3 mile; turn right and follow the drainage a few yards to the edge of the pool, although you will be across the river from the mouth of Bandy Creek.

The mouth of North White Oak Creek also has good fishing. Take the old O&W Railroad bed down from Verdun to the O&W Bridge; directions are given in the section on paddling. From there drive (at your own risk) or walk across the bridge and continue down the railbed a quarter mile or so until you can make your way down to North White Oak Creek. The pool in the river below the O&W Bridge has been good for smallmouth bass.

You'll also find good fishing at Blue Heron. On the drive down to the historic mining community, you'll notice pulloffs on the road where it parallels the river; you can park there to get down to the river. The Station Camp River Access at the end of Station Camp Road also offers access to the river for fishing.

The Clear Fork River with access at Burnt Mill Bridge, Brewster Bridge, and Peters Bridge has smallmouth bass. There are a number of small farm ponds on the rim area of the park; ask about those that might still be good for fishing. For example, you'll find smallmouth bass and bluegill in the pond down the hill from the Joe Branch Picnic Area; look for directions in the section on four-wheel driving.

The Big South Fork system is not particularly known for trout, which is not considered native; those you find today in tributary streams are remnant populations from stocking that occurred before the NPS took over the BSFNRRA. You can still find some trout in the Laurel Fork of Station Camp Creek, which you can reach along hiking and horse trails running between Bandy Creek and the Middle Creek areas. Trout are also in Rock Creek, which you can reach on hiking trails out of Pickett State Park or off Divide Road in the Middle Creek Area. Williams Creek also has some trout; take a horse trail leading northeast from the Station Camp East Trailhead to connect with a four-wheel drive road that runs north along a ridge to the west of Williams Creek.

Hiking and horseback riding will get you into the backcountry for fishing. Bandy Creek Stables offers guided horse rides and overnight camping for fishing trips with prior arrangement. Also the river outfitters can get you to good fishing spots.

Be careful while walking along the stream banks and while standing on boulders in the stream. The river can rise rapidly from a storm upstream, and boulders can be slippery and unstable. Copperheads like to sun on rocks along streams.

TRAPPING

At one time, trapping animals for furs was a way of obtaining supplemental income for those living on subsistence farms in the area. But trapping is no longer economically viable due to the low price for furs. Even so, trapping is allowed in the BSFNRRA subject to Tennessee and Kentucky regulations. You must have a license to trap for the state in which you are operating. Check with the Kentucky Department of Fish & Wildlife and the Tennessee Wildlife Resources Agency for the furbearer seasons, species limits, and other state regulations.

Typical furbearers found in the Big South Fork are mink, muskrat, beaver, opossum, red fox, gray fox, raccoon, weasel, bobcat, and striped skunk. River otters and spotted skunks are rare and must not be taken. Do not set traps on trails or in other areas that will be frequented by people. All traps must be visited once a day and any animals removed.

Visitor Participation

The BSFNRRA has a number of programs in which the public can participate, from educational presentations for schools groups and campfire talks for the park's overnight visitors to opportunities for the public to donate time and resources in support of the park. In addition, there are outside community and conservation groups working for the park that you may join and/or support. For the park's programs, contact the Bandy Creek Visitor Center for information. For outside groups, contact the individual group; addresses and phone numbers are listed in the back of this book.

ENVIRONMENTAL EDUCATION PROGRAM

The park staff provides a variety of programs in environmental education for school groups. Programs presented in area schools include archaeological resource protection, survival skills, litter problems, food chains and food webs, snakes, recycling, mammals, and fighting wild fires. Programs presented to school groups that come to the park include American Indian habitation, trees, river safety, clean water, and guided hikes introducing students to the park's resources. Schools and individual teachers may request these programs for their classes and may also ask for a program to be designed for their specific needs.

ENVIRONMENTAL EDUCATION CAMP

The park offers a three-day camp in the fall of each year for high school students. A variety of intellectually challenging programs presented during the camp help to develop an appreciation of the BSFNRRA and its natural resources and to support management issues and special initiatives at the park. The camp is designed to complement the school curriculum. Schools may request participation of selected students.

LONGHUNTER PROGRAM

A park ranger in traditional long hunter dress of the 1780s depicts the early exploration of the region. The long hunter discusses how a person or family group might survive in the open at a time when the only resources were the forest and what the people were able to bring with them. This program is available to school groups, scouts, and community groups and at times is presented at campfire programs.

Longhunter Program

CAMPFIRE PROGRAMS

Between Memorial Day and Labor Day, the park staff presents campfire programs every Friday and Saturday evening for visitors staying at the Bandy Creek Campground and any others who wish to attend. Depending on visitation patterns, the programs may continue into October. The programs range from talks about how to avoid ticks and other safety concerns, through presentations on the American long rifle and other historical topics, to storytelling. These programs are presented at the campfire amphitheater between Loops A and B in the campground or in the larger amphitheater north of the Bandy Creek Visitor Center, or at the Visitor Center itself if it is raining. Short talks are also sometimes presented during the day at the Visitor Center. The schedule for these programs is posted on campground bulletin boards and at the Visitor Center and advertised in area newspapers.

At this writing, a campfire program at the Blue Heron Campground awaits construction of an amphitheater or campfire circle where the programs can be held. Short talks are given at the mining community during the time the scenic train operates.

JUNIOR RANGER PROGRAM

Designed for 3-12 year olds, the Junior Ranger Program helps children learn about the National Park Service and the BSFNRRA. A child can pick up a handbook at either the Bandy Creek Visitor Center or at the Blue Heron Interpretive Center at the mining community. The fun activities in the handbook include hiking, attending programs, and visiting natural and cultural areas within the park. After completing the activities in the handbook, each child goes back to the Visitor Center or Blue Heron and talks with a ranger, who may ask questions to see what the child has learned. The child then receives an official Junior Ranger Badge.

PATCH HIKE

Groups such as Boy and Girl Scouts can receive a patch for doing a hike that includes the Oscar Blevins and John Litton Farm Loops and completing activities along the way. You can pick up the leader's guide and hiking guides for each member at the Visitor Center; these guides are also available to the general public. The leader's guide includes a form to be sent to the Great Smoky Mountains Council of the Boy Scouts in order to receive the patches.

SPECIAL EVENTS

Throughout the year, the park sponsors special events for the general visitor and for those participating in specialized outdoor activities. For the general visitor, the events might be pioneer encampments where volunteers demonstrate and explain the lifestyles and skills of the early pioneers. Or you can participate in the Cumberland Color Caper, a series of programs and activities focused on fall color that occurs the latter part of October. A number of special activities and programs are conducted in cooperation with the Big South Fork Scenic Railway.

Events for specific outdoor activities range from such happenings as a Mountain Bike Rally and the Blue Heron Run for runners and walkers, both held in late summer, to the Big South Fork Competitive Ride held in the spring for horseback riders to compete on handling and conditioning.

Pioneer encampment

Contact the Bandy Creek Visitor Center for a schedule of events and who to contact.

VIP PROGRAM

Volunteers in Park (VIP) is a way for groups and individuals to donate their time and skills in support of the BSFNRRA and its resources. The VIP Program has been instituted in just about every park in the National Park System. At the Big South Fork, individuals can work at the Visitor Center, do trail maintenance, adopt an area to monitor and take care of, present demonstrations and prepare special events, answer mail requests, give guided nature walks, help in producing inventories, serve as campground hosts. VIPs may work a few hours a week or month, seasonally, or full-time. To be a VIP, you must complete an application that asks about your talents, skills, and interests. Some interesting projects could be work in historical restoration and historical research if you have the required skills.

PARTNERS IN PARKS/PARTNERS IN EDUCATION

Partners in Parks or Partners in Education is a way for schools, businesses, and other groups to donate time and resources to support the park. Schools may work on educational projects, especially materials for interpretation. Businesses may donate materials, sponsor specific projects like the printing of brochures, and even donate the time of their employees to work in the park.

Under this program, the 1991 biology classes of Scott County High School assisted in the development of the self-guided tree-identification walk along the Angel Falls Trail and the accompanying brochure. At this writing, students of the Oneida Elementary School are at work on a guide to the Middle Creek Nature Trail.

BIG SOUTH FORK BICYCLE CLUB

This locally organized bicycle club helps promote bicycling in the Big South Fork. Members have participated in constructing mountain bike trails and in sponsoring the annual Mountain Bike Rally, which includes the Cumberland Mountain Bike Championship, the only mountain bike race held in a unit of the National Park System at this writing.

BIG SOUTH FORK TRAIL RIDERS ASSOCIATION

This association of horse riders supports trail riding in the park by raising money for trail maintenance and participating in trail clean up. Among their contributions was a donation of a horse to the park for rangers to use in patrolling the horse trails.

BIG SOUTH FORK SADDLE CLUB

Members of this club have been riding the trails in the Big South Fork area for over 25 years. The club will provide information and recommendations on the horse trails in the park if you contact them at the address listed in the back. Members also participate in clean up of trails and access roads.

BIG SOUTH FORK REGIONAL ASSOCIATION

This association has turned its attention first to promoting business and tourism development in the five-county region surrounding the park. But they also see their mission as promoting outdoor recreation and outdoor education in the region, especially in the park. They have proposed an outdoor adventure and education center that will work in cooperation with schools and universities to encourage study of the natural resources of the region.

TENNESSEE CITIZENS FOR WILDERNESS PLANNING

TCWP is the Tennessee conservation organization that was instrumental in the establishment of the BSFNRRA. In addition to being involved in various state and national conservation issues, the organization continues to work for the preservation of the Big South Fork, helping to ensure the authorizing legislation is adequately and wisely implemented and helping to see that the park receives adequate federal funding for land acquisition and operating expenses.

Visitor Participation

Surrounding Communities

Communities surrounding the BSFNRRA offer accommodations and a touch of history. You'll find here the descendents of the people of the Big South Fork and more recent arrivals ready to welcome visitors.

ONEIDA, TENNESSEE

Oneida was originally part of the community of Pine Creek. Then in the 1870s the Southern Railroad was built through the area, connecting Cincinnati with Chattanooga. A more populated community grew up near the rail line, and when a post office was established, the community was named for Oneida, New York; some of the investors in the railroad and community were from there and recognized the similarity of the area's rolling hills and stands of white pine.

Located at the junction of US27 and TN297, Oneida still supports lumbering and wood products industries. Just north of the junction, the headquarters of the old O&W Railroad still stands on the west side of US27, an elegant two-story brick building that now houses a chiropractic clinic; the Oneida O&W depot was located across the street where the First National Bank now stands. Contact the Scott County Chamber of Commerce (800/645-6905) for details on the motels and restaurants in Oneida and the surrounding communities.

JAMESTOWN, TENNESSEE

Located on the west side of the park, Jamestown was once the home of John Marshall Clemens, the father of Samuel Langhorne Clemens, who was the writer Mark Twain. It is said that Mark Twain was conceived in Jamestown, but the family moved to Missouri before he was born. You'll see references to Mark Twain in some of the signs in the area. A small park near the center of town protects the small spring from which the Clemens family got their water while living nearby.

North of the downtown area on old US127, you'll find the York Institute, founded by Sgt. Alvin C. York, the World War I hero, to educate the children of the region; you'll find on the campus the Mountaineer Craft Center with crafts on exhibit and for sale. You can continue north on US127 to York's hometown of Pall Mall. To the south, you can visit the Highland Manor Winery and sample their award-winning wines and tour the winery.

Jamestown is located at the junction of US127 and TN52. West of the town center on TN52, at the corner of Depot Lane, the old O&W Railroad depot, a large wooden structure built in 1930, still stands on the south side of the highway. Contact the Fentress County Chamber of Commerce (615/879-9948) for details on the restaurants and motels in Jamestown and surrounding communities. The Chamber is housed in a historic jail, built in 1898, located in Jamestown on TN52.

WHITLEY CITY, KENTUCKY

Originally the community of Coolidge, the town changed its name in 1912 to Whitley City when McCreary County was formed. It had been part of Whitley County, which had been named for Col. William Whitley, a frontiersman who was an early Indian fighter. Whitley City is located on US27 near the northern end of the BSFNRRA. Contact the McCreary County Chamber of Commerce (606/376-5004) for details on the restaurants and motels in Whitley City and surrounding communities.

RUGBY, TENNESSEE

Founded as the last English colony in the United States, Rugby served as a refuge where the second sons of English gentry, who had

Surrounding Communities

O&W Depot at Jamestown

no inheritance, could earn a living through farming and industry without sullying their families' reputations. The colony had been the idea of English author Thomas Hughes; he helped acquire land and encouraged immigration. The town took on the name of the English school Hughes had attended and which was the setting for his famous novel *Tom Brown's School Days*. Rugby was dedicated in 1880.

The town took shape as houses were built and a school, church, inn, and library were erected. The colony was never a great financial success. Most of the colonists eventually moved on to other opportunities.

In the 1960s, an association formed, now called "Historic Rugby, Inc.," that took over the management and preservation of many of the historic structures in the town. You'll find there today the old school, church, library, and several of the Victorian homes nestled in the forest of the Cumberland Plateau. Tours of the historic community begin at the visitor center, which is in the old school building. You can stay the night at Newbury Lodge, Pioneer Cottage, or Percy Cottage (for reservations call 615/628-2430) and have dinner at the Harrow Road Cafe. To the

Exploring the Big South Fork

Thomas Hughes Library at Rugby

west on TN52 there's also the Grey Gables Bed & Breakfast and the R. M. Brooks General Store and Post Office, a traditional rural store; south of TN52, the Clear Fork Farm Bed & Breakfast borders the southern portion of the BSFNRRA above the Clear Fork.

Rugby sits on TN52 between Elgin on US27 to the east and Jamestown on US127 to the west. The community borders the BSFNRRA on the south; it's about 35 miles from the Bandy Creek Visitor Center. Near the cemetery in the community, you can walk the Gentlemen's Swimming Hole Trail down to the Clear Fork River within the park.

ALLARDT, TENNESSEE

Founded soon after Rugby, Allardt was a German colony established by M. H. Allardt and Bruno Gernt. Allardt died shortly afterward, and the community was named for him. The Allardt colonists were more successful than those at Rugby in establishing an economic base in agriculture, mining, and timbering. But the remaining historic buildings of the present community are less extensive and less elaborate than those at Rugby, and so for that reason perhaps, the community remains less known. The town lies about 12 miles west of Rugby on TN52. You'll find in the community the Bruno Gernt House, built in 1881-1882 and now a bed and breakfast (615/879-8517). The Gernt family still manages the family's holdings from the Gernt Office, a small white building near the center of town. In addition to the Gernt House, they also have secluded log cabins for rent by the week or weekend.

STEARNS, KENTUCKY

Established in 1902 by Stearns Coal and Lumber, this company town grew up in the virtual wilderness to serve as the central point for the company's operations. The town was founded by William A. Kinne, land and timber agent for the company who lived in Stearns thereafter, and E. E. Barthell, the company's general counsel. The site they chose for the new town was a Southern Railroad siding and crosstie yard, locally called "Hemlock." The Stearns company created in the town the first entirely electric lumber yard in the country. To power the operation, the company constructed a steam power plant fueled by waste from the

Top: Bruno Gernt House
Bottom: Stearns 1919 (Courtesy of Stearns Museum)

lumber yard. In another innovative move, the steam from the power plant boilers was used to heat the offices, businesses, and executive residences and the resulting distilled water filled the town's water system. With divestiture that began in later years, Stearns was no longer a company town by 1977.

Stearns sits at the junction of KY92 and KY1651 west of US27. The Stearns Museum is housed in the old company headquarters that stands on a hill; the 1907 building also contained the town's bank. You'll find in the museum exhibits, old photos, and artifacts about the Stearns Company and other local history; the artifacts include the drill bit from the first commercial oil well, which was located on Martin Beaty's land now within the BSFNRRA. There's a small charge to tour the museum, which is open most days except Mondays during the spring, summer, and fall, but is closed late fall and winter.

In the middle of the town area stands a complex of buildings completed in the 1920s that once contained Stores No. 1 and No. 3 for groceries and hardware, plus the dentist's and doctor's offices. The McCreary County Heritage Foundation intends to restore the block of buildings and has recently received a grant to help with that project. A restaurant still occupies the old coffee shop. The theater or opera house is now the Kentucky (or Bear Creek) District Office of the BSFNRRA; this office is scheduled to move east of the town center to a location on KY92 closer to US27 and to then have visitor information, so watch for a possible change of location.

The site just to the northwest of the museum was the location of the hotel that was burned in 1908 to dislodge union organizers who had taken refuge there for fear of being arrested. The hotel was rebuilt after the fire but in later years was torn down. To the east once stood the community hall. Back in the community, you'll also find a golf course, one of the oldest in Kentucky.

The old structure along the railroad tracks and just to the east of the main block of buildings was the R. L. Stearns Wholesale Grocery warehouse. Robert L. Stearns, the son of company-founder Justus Stearns, took over company operations from his father; he had lived in Stearns in the early years and returned for a few months out of the year thereafter. His son, Robert L. Stearns, Jr., was a later president of the company and lived in Stearns most of his adult life.

Up the hill behind the Stearns Museum, the continuation of KY1651, you'll find the neighborhoods and houses where the company officials lived. Many of the wood frame houses date from 1910. The last Stearns family home is the large white house behind the museum.

A walking tour of Stearns is being prepared; ask at the museum for information. You'll find a few places of accommodation in Stearns, like the Big South Fork Motor Lodge and the Marcum-Porter House Bed and Breakfast.

Stearns is also the location of the Big South Fork Scenic Railway that provides train rides down into the Big South Fork Gorge to the Blue Heron Mining Community. The scenic railway presently operates out of the old rail yard of the Kentucky and Tennessee Railroad. You'll see there the old railcar repair building sitting in the midst of the yard, which was also the lumber yard; the lumber mill burned years ago. Future plans call for the train depot to move to the restored section of town and

Big South Fork Scenic Railway (Courtesy of Lavidge & Associates, Inc.)

Surrounding Communities

to be located in the old Stearns grocery warehouse once it is restored; so watch for the relocation. The scenic train ride following the route of the K&T along Roaring Paunch Creek is about 40 minutes one-way; the entire trip with layover at Blue Heron runs about 3 hours. There is a fare. The train operates most days April through October; inquire about the current schedule.

BARTHELL, KENTUCKY

Barthell was the first coal mining camp along the Kentucky and Tennessee Railroad. The camp was named for E. E. Barthell, the Stearns Coal and Lumber Company's general counsel who helped found Stearns, Kentucky. The first coal mined by the Stearns Company and shipped out of the watershed on the K&T came from Mine #1 at Barthell on June 1, 1903. The land for the community and the coal operations was originally leased by the Stearns company but was finally purchased in 1923. The small community once had a population of 300, consisting mainly of families. In addition to houses, the town included Stearns' Store No. 2, which included the post office. A schoolhouse that held classes nine months out of the year also doubled as the church. The tipple at Barthell burned in 1943, and the coal from that camp's mines was thereafter hauled to the Blue Heron Tipple.

As the coal camp was abandoned due to the slowdown in the industry, the community's structures were dismantled by the company during the period 1952-62, and the town disappeared except for a few foundations. But Barthell is slated for rebirth. A corporation lead by Harold Koger, a local resident whose family lived and worked in the region, has embarked on a grand project to recreate Barthell as it was in the 1920s and early 1930s. Phase one of the project will include reconstruction of nine houses, one log cabin, the schoolhouse, the store, and the old bathhouse within the historic area. You'll be able to tour the store, with all the tools and technology of the time, and one of the dwellings, containing typical furniture, clothes, and other articles used by the people of Barthell. The other houses will have authentic facades but will contain shops and overnight lodging. The historic area will eventually include the powder house where explosives were kept, the cap house that stored fuses, the electric substation, and more

Barthell Coal Camp (Courtesy of Stearns Museum)

dwellings. Outside of the historic area will be a restaurant and eventually an amphitheater, a railroad depot where the Big South Fork Scenic Railway will stop, boarding houses that will be bed and breakfasts, and shops and cabins. A replica of one of the mines is planned. On a visit, you'll enjoy picnicking, music, and getting a look at the way company towns of the time appeared.

The Barthell reconstruction will border the park. The first phase is scheduled to open in 1995. Watch for it, and contact the park's Visitor Center for information.

In addition to being able to ride the scenic railway to Barthell, you will also eventually be able to drive to the community. You'll take the Mine 18 Road down toward Blue Heron, and at 3 miles from the Bear Creek Scenic Area turnoff, or about 2 miles before Blue Heron, there will be a road to the right that leads to the community; at this writing, there's a rough dirt road that follows an old tramroad to the site. At the end of the road, you'll park and then walk a bridge across Roaring Paunch Creek into the historic section.

Surrounding Communities

Nearby Parks and Preserves

Although the BSFNRRA is the focus for outdoor activities in this part of the region, the surrounding area has a number of other parks and preserves where you can find additional opportunities for outdoor recreation.

PICKETT STATE RUSTIC PARK AND FOREST

Adjacent to the BSFNRRA on the western edge of the park in Tennessee, Pickett State Rustic Park and Forest possesses a similar geology. So you'll find here stone arches and rock shelters throughout the park and sandstone bluffs where Thompson Creek forms its own small canyon as it flows to meet Rock Creek that eventually joins the Big South Fork in Kentucky.

To get to the park, take TN297 west from the Bandy Creek Visitor Center to its junction with TN154. Turn north for 2.7 miles to the park entrance; you'll pass the road on the right into the Middle Creek area before the entrance.

There is no lodge in the park, but it does have chalets and cottages for rent year-round. The park's campground has 40 sites, and there's also a group camp with bathhouses, cabins, and a kitchen/dining lodge. Activities include picnicking, hiking the numerous trails, and swimming, boating, and fishing on the small lake created by the Thompson Creek Dam.

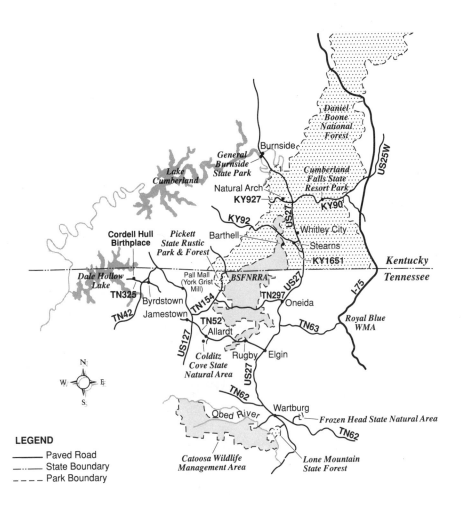

Communities and Parks Surrounding the Big South Fork

SGT. ALVIN C. YORK MEMORIAL GRIST MILL

This Tennessee state historic site commemorates Sgt. Alvin C. York, who while alone in a World War I battle in the Argonne Forest of France captured 132 German soldiers, killed 28, and so neutralized 35 machine-gun bunkers, for which he was awarded the Congressional Medal of Honor. A movie was later made of his exploits.

After returning to his home in Pall Mall, Tennessee, he operated the mill you can visit today. The historic site also includes the old York homeplace, a store and post office once owned by York, a Bible school he built, and the burial site of York.

To get to Pall Mall, head south on TN154 from the intersection with TN297. In 10 miles turn north on US127 and travel another 9 miles to the community.

Sergeant York Grist Mill

Exploring the Big South Fork

DALE HOLLOW LAKE AND CORDELL HULL BIRTHPLACE

If you're interested in lake boating and fishing, you can make your way to Dale Hollow Lake on the Obey River tributary of the Cumberland River west of the park. Continue on US127 north from Pall Mall for another 8 miles and turn west on TN42 and watch for several exits for lake access in the vicinity of Byrdstown. While you're in the area, you can also stop by the Cordell Hull Birthplace, an historic site on TN325, or Star Point Road, west off TN42. As Secretary of State, Hull authored the U.S. "Good Neighbor" policy and later received the Nobel Peace Prize.

DANIEL BOONE NATIONAL FOREST

Surrounding the northern part of the BSFNRRA in Kentucky, the Daniel Boone National Forest offers more opportunity for outdoor recreation. Hunting, fishing, four-wheel driving, hiking, horseback riding, camping, backpacking, and more are approved activities. The Sheltowee Trace National Recreation Trail travels south 257 miles through the national forest to enter the BSFNRRA and end at Pickett State Rustic Park on the west. Off KY1363 west of the park, the national forest has the Bell Farm Horse Camp with 5 campsites but no water or electricity. From the west end of KY1363, following the graveled FSR564 and then turning south on FSR137, you'll find the the Hemlock Grove Picnic Area and the Great Meadows Campground with 20 campsites and drinking water and pit toilets but no electricity. Farther down FSR137, a new Rock Creek Trailhead is proposed that will give access to the John Muir Trail, the Sheltowee Trace, and the Forest Service's Buffalo Arch Trail. An additional horse camp is planned for near Whitley City. Contact the Stearns Ranger District Office north of Whitley City on US27 for details.

CUMBERLAND FALLS STATE RESORT PARK

Surrounded by the Daniel Boone National Forest, Cumberland Falls State Resort Park lies north of the BSFNRRA. Head north on US27 to a right on KY90 that leads to the Kentucky state park, about a 20-mile drive north from Whitley City.

Cumberland Falls on the Cumberland River is the park's main

Cumberland Falls

attraction. This broad waterfall is sometimes called the "Niagara of the South." On clear, full-moon nights with plenty of water coming over the falls, you can see a moonbow—a rainbow that appears in the mist of the falls. It's sometimes claimed that this is the only moonbow in the Western Hemisphere, but there are several others. The park has a lodge, cabins, duplexes, swimming pool, tennis courts, and a campground with 50 sites for tents and trailers that have water and electric hookup.

NATURAL ARCH SCENIC AREA

On the way to Cumberland Falls, you can stop off at the national forest's Natural Arch Scenic Area to see one of the large natural sandstone arches found on the Cumberland Plateau. Just before the right turn on KY90, turn left on KY927 and drive to the entrance on the right in about 2 miles. You'll find picnicking and hiking trails that lead to the massive arch with a span of 100 feet and a clearance of 60 feet.

Natural Arch

GENERAL BURNSIDE STATE PARK AND LAKE CUMBERLAND

The most significant Civil War happening in the Big South Fork region occurred when President Lincoln ordered General Ambrose Burnside to invade East Tennessee from Kentucky. Rather than attempting a pass through Cumberland Gap, which was held by the Confederates at the time, Burnside marched his troops through the Big South Fork country. Burnside, Kentucky, and General Burnside State Park are named in his honor.

Twenty miles north of Whitley City on US27, you'll find a causeway that leads to the island park located where the Big South Fork joins the Cumberland River. This recreation park has a swimming pool, golf course, and a campground with 110 sites for tents and trailers with electric and water hookups. You can use the park to fish and explore the waters of Lake Cumberland.

COLDITZ COVE STATE NATURAL AREA

This 75-acre Tennessee state natural area contains 60-foot Northrup Falls set in a cove of hemlock and rhododendron. A mile-long loop trail takes you behind the waterfall. Rudolph and Arnold Colditz donated the land for the natural area to the state. The waterfall is named for a family that once lived at the head of the falls. The trail was constructed by the Cumberland Chapter of the Tennessee Trails Association.

Eleven miles west of Rugby on TN52, just inside the town limits of Allardt, turn south on the Crooked Creek Road and drive one mile to parking and the trailhead on the right.

OBED WILD AND SCENIC RIVER

To the south, the Obed River carves a deep gorge in the surface of the Cumberland Plateau, creating a similar topography to the Big South Fork Gorge. Designated a national wild and scenic river in 1976, the river has become known as one of the best whitewater rivers in the southeast. Paddlers value the wilderness experience along the isolated 45 miles of the river corridor that include stretches along the tributaries, Clear Creek and Daddys Creek. The difficulty ranges from II to V and so

Northrup Falls at Colditz Cove State Natural Area

Obed Wild and Scenic River

the runs are for experienced paddlers only. There is a picnic area at Nemo Bridge on the Emory River near the Obed's junction with the Emory.

The wild and scenic river is managed under the direction of the BSFNRRA superintendent. The visitor center is located in the town of Wartburg, which was originally a German colony founded in 1848. Take US27 south from Oneida. Wartburg is about 50 miles from the BSFNRRA Bandy Creek Visitor Center.

The Obed passes through the Catoosa Wildlife Management Area, an 80,000-acre preserve managed by the Tennessee Wildlife Resources Agency. Hunting and fishing are popular activities. The Obed River Gorge also offers plenty of opportunity for climbing and rappelling.

FROZEN HEAD STATE NATURAL AREA

Near the Obed Wild and Scenic River, Frozen Head State Natural Area provides more opportunity for hiking and backpacking in its 11,869 acres that includes Frozen Head Mountain. From Wartburg, take TN62 southeast 4 miles to a turn north on a paved road that leads 2 miles to the natural area. About 50 miles of trails wander the area. There's also picnicking and tent camping. Register at the visitor center for overnight camping in the backcountry.

LONE MOUNTAIN STATE FOREST

This Tennessee state forest offers hiking, horseback riding, and hunting among its outdoor activities. Located in the vicinity of Frozen Head State Park and the Obed Wild and Scenic River, Lone Mountain State Forest lies to the west of US27; 4 miles southeast of Wartburg, turn right on Clayton Howard Road to enter the forest.

ROYAL BLUE WILDLIFE MANAGEMENT AREA

This newly established Tennessee WMA is accessible at the TN63 exit off I-75. The area lies east of I-75 and west along TN63 as you head for the BSFNRRA west from the interstate. Managed by the Tennessee Wildlife Resources Agency, this preserve shelters an open hardwood

Emory Gap Falls at Frozen Head State Natural Area

forest that lies on the eastern edge of the Cumberland Plateau; a reclamation project will rehabilitate abandoned strip mines in the area. Activities here include hunting, fishing, hiking, mountain biking, horseback riding, and four-wheel and ATV driving. Motorized vehicles, horses, and bicycles must only use existing roads. A special ATV area is planned, and camping will be allowed in designated camping areas.

Addresses and Telephone Numbers

Backwoods Adventures
P.O. Box 366
Oneida, TN 37841-0366
615/569-9573

Bandy Creek Stables
P.O. Box 191
Huntsville, TN 37756
615/879-4013

Big South Fork Bicycle Club
P.O. Box 4129
Oneida, TN 37841
615/569-4080

Big South Fork National River and
Recreation Area
Rt. 3 Box 401
Oneida, TN 37841
615/879-3625 or 879-4890
(Bandy Creek Visitor Center)
615/569-9778 (Park Headquarters)
606/376-3787
(Blue Heron Mining Community)

Big South Fork Regional Association
P.O. Box 309
Allardt, TN 38504
615/879-2809

Big South Fork Saddle Club
Rt. 2, Box 250B
Oneida, TN 37841

Big South Fork Scenic Railway
P.O. Box 368
Stearns, KY 42647
800/462-5664
606/376-5330

Big South Fork Trail Riders Association
P.O. Box 4457
Oneida, TN 37841

Bruno Gernt House
Estate of Bruno Gernt
P.O. Box 69
Allardt, TN 38504
615/879-8517

Charit Creek Lodge
250 Apple Valley Road
Sevierville, TN 37862
615/429-5704

Cumberland Falls State Resort Park
Rt. 6, Box 411
Corbin, KY 40701
606/528-4121

Cumberland Rapid Transit
Box 200, Rock Creek Route
Jamestown, TN 38556
615/879-4818

Fentress County Ambulance
615/879-8147

Fentress County Chamber
of Commerce
P.O. Box 1294
Jamestown, TN 38556
615/879-9948

Fentress County General Hospital
W. Central Avenue
Jamestown, TN
615/879-8171

Frozen Head State Natural Area
Rt. 2, Box 1302
Wartburg, TN 37887
615/346-3318

General Burnside State Park
P.O. Box 488
Burnside, KY 42519-0488
606/561-4104

Historic Rugby, Inc.
P.O. Box 8
Rugby, TN 37733
615/628-2430

Kentucky Department of Fish and
Wildlife Resources
#1 Game Farm Road
Frankfort, KY 40601
502/564-4336

McCreary County Ambulance
606/376-5062

McCreary County Chamber
of Commerce
P.O. Box 548
Whitley City, KY 42653
606/376-5004

Obed Wild and Scenic River
P.O. Box 429
Wartburg, TN 37887
615/346-6295

Pickett State Rustic Park
State Hwy. 154
Jamestown, TN 38556
615/879-5821

Scott County Chamber of Commerce
P.O. Box 4442
Oneida, TN 37841
800/645-6905
615/569-6900

Scott County Ambulance
615/569-6000

Scott County Hospital
Hwy US27
Oneida, TN
615/569-8521

Scott County Sheriff
Huntsville, TN
615/663-2245

Sheltowee Trace Outfitters
P.O. Box 1060
Whitley City, KY 42653
800/541-RAFT

Stearns Museum
P.O. Box 452
Stearns, KY 42647
606/376-5730

Stearns Ranger District
Daniel Boone National Forest
P.O. Box 429
Whitley City, KY 42653
606/376-5323

Tennessee Citizens for Wilderness
    Planning
130 Tabor Road
Oak Ridge, TN 37830

Tennessee Wildlife Resources
    Agency
Wildlife Division
P.O. Box 40747
Nashville, TN 37204
800/262-6704

U.S. Army Corp of Engineers
(Flow Readings)
615/736-5455

Addresses and Telephone Numbers

Selected References

Blevins, Laccie W., and Ray E. Blevins. 1982. *Jonathan Blevins Sr. of Virginia and His Descendants.* Johnson City: The Overmountain Press.

Birdwell, Michael E. 1990. *Coal Mining in the Big South Fork Area of Kentucky and Tennessee.* Cookeville: Tennessee Technological University.

Des Jean, Tom. Unpublished paper. "Prehistory—Introduction and Conceptual Framework," National Park Service, BSFNRRA.

————. Draft manuscript. "Nineteenth Century Burial Practices of the Upper Cumberland Plateau," National Park Service, BSFNRRA.

Fiegel, Kurt H. Unpublished paper. "Disputing the Titusville Myth." Research on the first oil well.

Howell, Benita J. 1981. *A Survey of Folklife Along the Big South Fork of the Cumberland River.* Knoxville: The University of Tennessee.

Humphrey, Steve E. 1981. "The History of the No Business and Station Camp Communities," unpublished manuscript, National Park Service, BSFNRRA.

Hutchinson, Steven K., et al. 1982. *An Inventory and Evaluation of Architectural and Engineering Resources of the BSFNRRA.* Lexington: Environment Consultants, Inc.

Jones, James B. 1987. *The Development of Coal Mining on Tennessee's Cumberland Plateau, 1880-1930,* Study Unit #6. Nashville: State Historic Preservation Office.

Manning, Russ. 1993. *The Historic Cumberland Plateau, An Explorer's Guide.* Knoxville: The University of Tennessee Press.

————and Sondra Jamieson. 1990. *The Best of the Big South Fork, A Hiker's Guide to Trails and Attractions.* Norris, TN: Mountain Laurel Place.

McBride, Kim A. 1993. *A Background Archival and Oral Historical Study of the Barthell Coal Camp, McCreary County, Kentucky.* Lexington: University of Kentucky.

National Park Service. 1993. *Roads and Trails Management Plan Draft.* BSFNRRA.

————. No date. *A Guide to Paddling in the Big South Fork.* BSFNRRA.

————. "Big South Fork National River and Recreation Area Cemetery Inventory," unpublished report, 1989-90, BSFNRRA, Resource Management Division.

Perry, L. E. 1979. *McCreary Conquest: A Narrative History.* Whitley City: Published by the author.

Perry, Samuel D. 1983. *South Fork Country.* Detroit: Harlo Press.

Shepherd, Russell G. 1988. "America's First Commercial Oil Well." *Earth Sciences History*, Vol. 1, No. 2, pp. 134-139.

Smith, H. Clay. 1985. *Dusty Bits of the Forgotten Past, A History of Scott County.* Oneida: The Scott County Historical Society.

Stanley, Steven M. 1986. *Earth and Life Through Time.* New York: W. H. Freeman and Co.

Thomas, J. Patrick. 1989. *Lore & Legend, History Magazine*, Vol. 1 No. 1. Devoted to the history of the Stearns Coal & Lumber Company.

U.S. Army Corps of Engineers. 1986. *Structural Treatment Plan, National Register Eligible Architectural Structures, BSFNRRA.* Nashville.

————. 1976. *Big South Fork General Design Memorandum* and *Final Environmental Impact Statement.* Nashville.

Index

Index

The Historic Cumberland Plateau
An Explorer's Guide
by Russ Manning

Published by the University of
Tennessee Press

(paper $14.95, hardcover $29.95)

Here is Russ Manning's complete guide to the history and the outdoors of the Cumberland Plateau in Tennessee, Kentucky, Georgia, and Alabama. *The Historic Cumberland Plateau* provides the background to this Southeast region that includes the Big South Fork National River and Recreation Area.

Manning guides you through such places in Kentucky as Cumberland Gap National Historical Park, Pine Mountain, Daniel Boone National Forest, Red River Gorge, and Cumberland Falls State Park. In Tennessee, he takes you to the Big South Fork, Historic Rugby, the Obed Wild and Scenic River, Cumberland Homesteads, Sequatchie Valley, Fall Creek Falls State Park, Savage Gulf, the South Cumberland Recreation Area, and Lookout Mountain. He also takes you through Little River Canyon in Alabama and Cloudland Canyon in Georgia.

This new guidebook not only provides the historical background but also gives specific directions on how to explore each region and the locations of inns and bed & breakfasts and campgrounds; in addition, the book briefly describes the hiking and walking trails for each region. This guidebook provides information on state and national parks and recreation areas, state natural areas, and state forests and wildlife management areas throughout the region and gives directions to such natural wonders as the Plateau's canyons, waterfalls, natural arches, and caves. An introductory chapter gives the historical overview, explains the geology, and describes the plants and animals of the Cumberland Plateau. (360 pages, 16 maps, 66 photographs)

An essential guidebook for visitors to the Big South Fork and the Cumberland Plateau and for all those who enjoy regional history and the outdoors.

Order directly from the University of Tennessee Press (293 Communications Building, Knoxville, TN, 37996-0325, 615/974-3321) or from Mountain Laurel Place using the order form at the back.

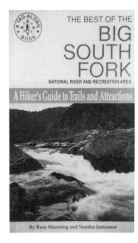

THE BEST OF THE
BIG
SOUTH
FORK
NATIONAL RIVER AND RECREATION AREA

A Hiker's Guide to Trails and Attractions

By Russ Manning and Sondra Jamieson

The Best of the Big South Fork
A Hiker's Guide to Trails and Attractions
2nd Edition
by Russ Manning and Sondra Jamieson

Published by Mountain Laurel Place

$6.95
Ask about an updated and expanded
3rd Edition available soon from Mountain
Laurel Place

Once you've been introduced to the Big South Fork National River and Recreation Area through *The Big South Fork Handbook*, you'll want to explore the park more thoroughly using Russ and Sondra's trail guide.

This second edition of *The Best of the Big South Fork* covers 32 favorite trails in the BSFNRRA and in the surrounding Pickett State Park, Daniel Boone National Forest, Rugby, and Colditz Cove State Natural Area. Each trail description includes the distance, difficulty, elevation loss or gain, cautions, trail connections, attractions, trailhead directions, and a detailed description of what you'll encounter along the trail. The guidebook also contains sections on geology, human history, plants and animals, and park history.

The 3rd Edition of the book promises to cover every hiking trail in the park and many of the horse trails. It will also include an indication of proposed trails to be constructed over the next several years. Watch for publication in 1995.

Order from Mountain Laurel Place using the order form at the back.

Other Books from Mountain Laurel Place

The Best of the Great Smoky Mountains, A Hiker's Guide to Trails and Attractions, by Russ Manning and Sondra Jamieson—a guide to the Great Smoky Mountains National Park in Tennessee and North Carolina, 256 pp., 4 1/2" x 7 1/2", $10.95

Tennessee's South Cumberland, A Hiker's Guide to Trails and Attractions, 2nd Edition, by Russ Manning and Sondra Jamieson—a guide to Tennessee's South Cumberland Recreation Area and Fall Creek Falls State Park, also on the Cumberland Plateau, 128 pp., 4 1/2" x 7 1/2", $7.95

Historic Knoxville and Knox County, A Walking and Touring Guide, by Russ Manning and Sondra Jamieson—a guide to the historic city center, neighborhoods, parks, and backroads of this Tennessee city and county, 256 pp., 4 1/2" x 7 1/2", $4.95 (Regular $8.95)

ORDER FORM

TITLE	PRICE	QTY.	TOTAL
The Historic Cumberland Plateau, An Explorer's Guide (paper)	$14.95		
The Historic Cumberland Plateau, An Explorer's Guide (cloth)	$29.95		
The Best of the Big South Fork, 2nd Edition	$ 6.95		
The Best of the Great Smoky Mountains	$10.95		
Tennessee's South Cumberland, 2nd Edition	$ 8.95		
Historic Knoxville and Knox County	$ 4.95		
Exploring the Big South Fork, A Handbook	$15.95		
	Subtotal		
	TN residents add 8.25% sales tax		
	Shipping and handling*		
	Total Enclosed		

*Add $2.00 for shipping and handling if ordering one book or for each book if separate mailing is requested. **We pay for shipping/handling if more than one book is ordered and mailed in one shipment to the same address.**

Mail check for total amount to:

Mountain Laurel Place
P.O. Box 3001
Norris, TN 37828
(615/494-8121)

Ship to: _____
Address: _____
City: _____ State: _____ Zip: _____

Items offered subject to availability. Prices subject to change without notice.